FINDING MORE TIME
IN YOUR LIFE

DRU SCOTT DECKER

HARVEST HOUSE PUBLISHERS
Eugene, Oregon 97402

Cover by Terry Dugan Design, Minneapolis, Minnesota

Portions of this material were previously published as How to Put More Time in Your Life (New York, NY: Rawson Associates, 1980).

FINDING MORE TIME IN YOUR LIFE
Copyright © 2001 by Dru Scott Decker
Published by Harvest House Publishers
Eugene, Oregon 97402

Library of Congress Cataloging-in-Publication Data
  Decker, Dru Scott
      Finding more time in your life / Dru Scott Decker
      p. cm.
      ISBN 0-7369-0307-0
      1. Time management—Religious aspects—Christianity.   2. Title.
  BV4598.5.D43 2001
  640′.43—dc21   2001016757

Printed in the United States of America

     01   02   03   04   05   06   07   / BP-CF/   10   9   8   7   6   5   4   3   2   1

For Bert,
*Whose competence and skill are a
delight and an inspiration.*

Acknowledgments

So many people have made this book possible they cannot be mentioned by name: The clients I have worked for and who provided the laboratory for testing so many of the ideas. The people in audiences and seminars who have shared their stories and who appear in cases. (Most of the time, their names have been changed to protect their privacy.) The colleagues who have opened the doors.

Charlie "Tremendous" Jones not only encouraged me but also called Bob Hawkins Jr., president of Harvest House Publishers, and said, "You have to talk to Dru Scott Decker."

Many friends and family members have been my cheerleaders and prayer friends, encouraging me in many different ways in person and in writing: Allison Sumpter; Clark Robinson; Dianna Booher; Elizabeth Paeth Lasker, MD; Fred Lasker, MD; Gail Castro; George Castro; Jusy Hester; Judy Jackson; Jennifer Tan; Kathy Trowbridge; Marilee Goodykoontz; Mary Butler; Pamela Lloyd Coates; Peggie Robinson; Peter F. Drucker; Stacey Padrick; Sue Halter; Thena Holman; Vicki Choy.

I would also like to acknowledge the Publisher's Committee at Harvest House Publishers, who sent me a ticket and invited me to sit around a table and talk with them: Bob Hawkins Jr., Carolyn McCready, Terry Glaspey, John Constance, LaRae Weikert, and Julie McKinney. Thanks also to my editor, Kim Moore, who deserves a bouquet of roses every day of the week, and the total team at Harvest House who provide such red carpet treatment, including Betty Fletcher, Barb Sherrill, Carol Ann Hickman, Hope Lyda, Kari Vorvick, Kathi MacKenzie-Foster, Katie Lane, Mary Cooper, Pat Mathis, Peggy Wright, Rebecca Santin, Stacy Hausler, and Teresa Evenson.

Contents

Part IV: Overcoming Tools—To Gain Energy and Get Back on Track

Part V: Daily Tools—For Success with Everyday Time Demands

Part VI: Spiritual Tools—For Enjoying Your Coach and Counselor

Preface

For I am confident of this very thing, that He who began a good work in you will perfect it until the day of Christ Jesus.

Philippians 1:6 NASB

Tools started to fascinate me when I was four. I used to watch my father construct carpentry projects at his worktable in the back of our garage. Even though he later became an invalid, the image of him I remember most was when he was standing and working at his table while I was sitting and watching from the small wooden bench he had built just for me. He would sketch the cupboard or chest he needed to build, and then he would reach for just the right tool for the task at hand.

That's what this book is. It's a means to help you sketch what needs be to built in your personal, professional, or spiritual life, and it's a collection of tools to help you with each task at hand.

As my father worked at his carpentry table, there were joyful moments when he would let me hold a board steady while he sawed or blow away curls of pinewood shavings. Something was special about those times with him. It was the thrill of joining my father in what he was doing. Being part of his team.

That's also what this book is about—joining our heavenly Father in what He is doing. When we concentrate on God's priorities, we grow in the freedom to put aside the dozens of pressures and priorities our culture piles on us. We can say no with confidence. We can work with direction. We can find more time. We can do it because we are not facing time challenges alone. We are on the right team.

Dru Scott Decker

Part I

The Strong Foundation

Starting with God

STARTING WITH GOD

- 🐚 When you want to find more time, don't try to do it alone.

- 🐚 Start with God. Ask Him to be your Coach and "Wonderful Counselor." Ask for God's help, and then follow His guidance.

Chapter 1

The People Side of Time Management and the Power of a Coach

He will be called Wonderful Counselor, Mighty God, Everlasting Father, Prince of Peace.
Isaiah 9:6

If you were to walk up to me and ask, "What are the best ways for finding more time?" my answers might surprise you. A few years ago, my first response would have been to encourage you to unplug your television, write your life purpose, and invest 15 minutes a day in an important project that has been collecting dust. These tools are still helpful, but now my first response is different. The best way to find more time in your life is: Get a great coach.

This isn't the personal coach you find in the yellow pages or on the Internet. The coach I'm recommending is the One I ignored for years. And even when I came to know Him personally, I still didn't talk with Him about my time. I thought He was only interested in huge events like hurricanes and earthquakes. It didn't seem possible He could care about things in my day like getting across town during rush hour, a flood of interruptions, or the stack of tough tasks that were screaming to be done.

Yet I have come to discover that talking with God *about* my time is the best help for my time. Talking with God removes the trap of: "I'm facing this alone." It adds the truth: "I can always turn to my Good Shepherd" (see John 10:11).

Listening to God in the Bible cuts the stress of wondering what to do. It reminds us we can count on the coaching and wisdom of our "Wonderful Counselor." It helps us walk in the light of His love and guidance.

The Right Coach

God is the right coach to help you with your time. As you read the collection of practical and positive ideas in this book, you can ask your Wonderful Counselor to coach you and guide you in finding the principles and tools that are right for you now. Ask Him to help you use them at the right times. And thank Him for His love, because He cares about you, your time, and everything in your day.

In addition to benefiting from the greatness of God's wisdom, you will benefit from the *personalized* time tools you will see.

When people walk into a clothing store, most step away from the sections that say, "One Size Fits All." It's the same when they look for resources to help with their time. Most people want personalized resources that fit their individual needs, pressures, and priorities.

When you find the few tools that are right for you, you will cut time pressures and make a difference. This combination of wisdom from the Bible and personalized tools will help you find more time in your life through doing the right things at the right times with God's help.

The Spiritual Side

Even though spiritual issues in a book on time may be different, I've now discovered that the spiritual side of life is what puts more life into your time. However, the beginning of this spiritual search came when I least expected it.

As the driver opened the door of the black limousine and I rushed to get in, the last thought in my mind was prayer, God, or guidance.

When I collapsed onto the backseat, I couldn't understand what had gone wrong. This morning had been a dream come true. Good things do come in threes! The selection by the Book-of-the-Month-Club of my new book. The strong advance sales for it. And the interview on *Good Morning America*.

Yet when the driver seated himself behind the wheel, looked back, touched his hat in salute, and offered, "You must feel on top of the world," I nodded yes, but if I were honest, I felt no. After working so hard to accomplish all of this, I was sure I would feel on top of the world. But I didn't. I had thought that all of this success would satisfy. But it didn't. I had dreamed that after a set of hard accomplishments like these, I would finally feel fulfilled. But I didn't. Life was not turning out the way I had dreamed.

As the driver continued down the avenue, I thought back to my childhood and how accomplishing tough things became my motivating force.

I remembered the admiration I felt for one of my mother's accomplishments. Many nights when I was growing up and in bed, I would hear her bedroom door squeak as she opened it. She would walk across the hall to the hospital bed where my father lay paralyzed, and she would move him so that he wouldn't get bedsores. She did this every day, every night, every two hours...and she did it for seven years.

When I was growing up, three days each year were the best. They were the days when I got off the school bus, walked up the gravel driveway to our house, and put my report card on the kitchen table to show my accomplishments. The time in the schoolbooks paid off.

As I sat in the backseat of the limousine and thought over the six years since setting up my own company, I realized my life had continued to be centered around books and accomplishments and little else.

I knew how to focus and squeeze the most out of each minute. People looked to me with questions, and I enjoyed giving my answers. On the radio. On television. In newspapers. And in books. It seemed as though everyone wanted my opinion.

Now, as I sat slumped in the back of the chauffeured car, my mind recounted the situation. My book on time was a success. The publicity was a success. I was a success. So why didn't I feel like a success? My time, while it delivered accomplishments, still left me unfulfilled.

As the limousine turned the corner toward the Plaza Hotel, I felt for the first time the deep emptiness in my life. Something was missing. Perhaps it was meaning. Or more significance. Definitely something different.

As the driver stopped in front of the hotel, opened my door, and helped me out, I realized I had to step in a new direction.

Someone Who Seemed Fulfilled

A saying I had heard flashed into my mind: Seek and you will find. I hoped that strategy would work even when I didn't even know what I was seeking. But I did know someone who seemed fulfilled and peaceful.

So the Saturday after I returned to San Francisco, I went for an early morning walk along the ocean with my neighbor and friend who had asked me out for occasional Saturday breakfasts and events during the last six years.

As Elizabeth Paeth Lasker, MD, and I walked along the misty beach, I posed the concern that was gnawing at me. "Even with all that I have done and all the wonderful things in my life, something is still missing. I feel spiritually flat. Unfulfilled. Empty. What should I do?"

Elizabeth continued walking along the sand for a moment, and then she turned and looked at me. She paused a moment more and looked into my eyes as if to make sure I wanted to listen to what she had to say. (My track record for being open to advice definitely had some holes in it.)

However, I had seen the gold medal the U.S. Surgeon General had presented to her, so I was sure I was going to receive something worthwhile.

But I was surprised and even a little disappointed at what she prescribed. True, I had never tried it, but I was hoping for something a little more mysterious. More profound. Perhaps a pilgrimage.

Her prescription was this: "You have discovered that your priorities are not enough. You are now searching for priorities from God."

The Prescription

I stood still as she let me think, and then she continued, "If you will pray and read something in the Bible every day for a year, you will not feel spiritually flat."

Then she invited me to stop by her house that afternoon so she could give me a gift. I unwrapped it to find a book with a gold cover: a *Good News Bible* with easy-to-read English and line sketches. After I opened her gift, she showed me a prayer that began "Our Father in heaven" (Matthew 6:9 TEV), and she showed me the table of contents where she had put a check mark in front of six sections: Psalms, Proverbs, Matthew, Mark, Luke, and John. Then she suggested that I might enjoy reading from those sections first. She encouraged me to read with the objective of understanding more of the character of God.

I had never done this before, and I didn't see much value in doing it now. But I admired Elizabeth, and I knew my answers weren't working. So after I thought about it, I agreed. It wouldn't be too hard to pray and read at least one sentence a day. After all, this would only take a couple of minutes each morning.

However, her six check marks seemed too structured for me. So I used the fan-and-finger method for a few days. Fan the book open. Drop the finger onto a random page. Then read the sentence I touched. Elizabeth had not recommended this method, and it didn't give me much context for what I was reading, so after a while I returned to the six sections she had marked.

I didn't realize what those three minutes a day of reading and praying would bring. In the weeks and months after this, I can remember a number of nights getting into bed, putting my head on the pillow, and then remembering, "I didn't pray and read something in the Bible today." I would pull myself out of bed, pray, and read a sentence or two.

At the end of a few months, I found that I was recalling things I had read in the Bible. For example, as I stood in front of an elevator, waiting and worrying about a meeting, I was pleasantly surprised as something I had read recently floated through my thoughts:

> Do not be afraid, little flock, for your Father is pleased to give you the Kingdom (Luke 12:32 TEV).

The words "give" and "gave" continued to touch me as I read other sentences in the Bible:

> For God loved the world so much that he gave his only Son, so that everyone who believes in him may not die but have eternal life (John 3:16 TEV).

Before I started reading the Bible, I had told a friend over dinner that I had done so many good things I was sure God would be glad to have me as part of His team. My friend, who had never read the Bible either, agreed. But as I kept on reading my "something" in the Bible each day, and as I prayed, I started to see things from a very different perspective.

I had hoped that at the end of my life there would be a scene with a big set of scales. One side would hold the bad things I had done. The other, the good things. I had hoped that God would look at both sides and say, "More good than bad. Come on in." However, the more I read the Bible, the more I saw this wasn't true.

Not a Grade to Be Earned

The spotlight was not on what I had done; it was on what God had done for me and whether I had accepted what He wanted to give me. As I kept on reading, I was surprised by other aspects of the character of God.

I had thought I had to earn God's love, but I read that it is a gift. I do not have to accomplish to earn it (Romans 6:23).

I had thought that God was a strict schoolteacher in the sky who had a ruler ready to rap my knuckles. Then I read that He is my Good Shepherd. I could rest (Psalm 23).

I had thought the Bible was a dusty book of "thee's" and "thou's" with little relationship to life today. I discovered that the

Bible is a treasure chest of wisdom and practical guidance for my life (Psalm 19:7-11).

I had thought that God loved a mass of nameless people until I read that He loves individuals, including me. I do not have to earn my value (Matthew 10:29-31).

The Pivotal Day

Then one routine day in my life turned into the pivotal day of my life. When I walked into a Gothic cathedral downtown and sat in a pew, I didn't realize how reading the Bible had helped me to see life in a different light, and how much it had taught me about the character of God. As I sat in the pew, gazing at the cross in the front of the cathedral, I was struck by the realization that God viewed my actions in a different way than I did. He called some things I was doing by very different names than I was calling them.

Suddenly, I understood that what I had been doing had fallen painfully short of what God designed me to be doing. For the first time I felt overwhelming grief for things I had done, and I asked God to forgive me.

When I finally walked to the front of the cathedral and knelt at the altar, my eyes settled on the high stained-glass windows. Rays of red, gold, blue, and purple light filtered down and made a silhouette of the priest who was standing before me.

He placed a small, broken piece of bread in my hands and said, "This is the body of Christ, which is broken for you."

For the first time, I understood that the body of Christ was broken not only for a mass of nameless people. The body of Christ was broken for me. He loved me. He knew my name.

I started to sense the incredible price He paid on the cross with His body to pay for my wrongdoing and to give me a relationship with the pure and holy God. A deep sense of the love of Jesus swept over me.

I now knew that I could trust God, and for the first time, I asked Him not just to help me—but to direct me.

From that day forward, my life began to change. My relationship with work changed, because I stopped seeking my value from accomplishments. My relationship with fame changed, because I realized it was a plus and not a necessity. My relationship with wealth changed, because I stopped confusing my net worth with my self-worth.

I had thought that accomplishing *any* objective would satisfy. I learned that the only objectives that will satisfy are the ones that please God.

Now, after that spiritual search, I know that in every personal issue and time issue, I am not alone. At every moment God is with me: the "Good Shepherd," the "Eternal Father," the "Wonderful Counselor," and the *Powerful Coach*.

Starting with God serves as the foundation for everything in this book. He is the starting place for growth, healing, and finding more time in your life.

Chapter 2

How This Book Can Help You

There is a time for everything, and a season for every activity under heaven: a time to be born and a time to die, a time to plant and a time to uproot, a time to kill and a time to heal, a time to tear down and a time to build.

Ecclesiastes 3:1-3

This book is different from any other book I've been involved with. When I first sat down to work on it, it was special. It was a book I almost had to write, because so many books on effectiveness and organization are written by people who are highly organized for people who are also highly organized. There needed to be something for the rest of us.

Have you ever experienced the pain of wanting to do something, knowing it is the best thing to do, and then falling short? If you have, you particularly understand the exhilarating sense of relief and joy in finding help to master something important in your life. For most of my life, I dashed breathlessly from one panic or crisis to the next. Although I have learned to use the tools in this book, it is an old pattern I need to continue to check.

If, like me, you have ever spent an extended period of time in rushing, disorganization, or chaos, you know the comfort of having a practical, powerful, enjoyable, ongoing program to find more time.

Some of the material on how to apply the ideas may seem very detailed. Remember that I'm writing for the tough cases like myself—the person who is often resistant to doing what is best for them.

Time In and Time Out

This book is not just to help you have highly productive and energetic times. It is also to help you have more balance. Enjoy productive, purposeful time periods—Time In—with equally important periods of total rest—Time Out. The Time Out helps you recharge your batteries. It's a vital process when you want to be enthusiastic and effective during your Time In. God didn't call it Time Out, but He did create a day of rest.

In this book you will learn specific and practical techniques to deal with nagging time problems. You will learn how to achieve your objectives faster, and you will discover important behavioral insights that will help you to move beyond the limitations of traditional time programs.

Past Solutions May Not Be Enough

Time pressures are skyrocketing at an alarming pace for millions of people, and many haven't been told that God cares about them individually, cares about their time, and cares about everything in their lives. Even people who are followers of Christ may hesitate asking for God's help with the details of their time even though God has numbered the hairs on their head. In the face of time pressures, they may forget the reality that they matter to God.

Many people are embarrassed to have started a time-improvement program and then let it drop. They are relieved to know that most time improvements take ongoing reinforcement and repetition. Fortunately, God is a God of new beginnings.

Many people also handcuff themselves with the expectation that they have to do everything and do it to perfection. What a relief to reinforce that God doesn't want us to do everything. He helps us to do the right things, and do them at the right times, with His power.

Because People Complicate Your Time

One way this book can help you is through its focus on the people side of your time. The process of enriching and enhancing your time has complications. For most of us, learning how to use time to do what is most productive, healthy, and satisfying requires much more than the cold and impersonal techniques common to traditional time tools. These traditional methods don't work for many people because they ignore a basic reality. Most of us are not in a position to ignore others in our lives. We can't shut the door, sit at a desk, and have hours of uninterrupted planning. We have friends, parents, children, spouses, bosses, coworkers, customers, and employees. They make demands on our time, and we have responsibilities to them. And who wants to be an isolated lighthouse keeper anyway? At least not on most days.

In addition, most of us are not willing to exploit every contact with people and every moment in selfish pursuit of our objectives. We want more from our time, but we're also concerned with others' feelings. We want to be a cooperative team player, not a lone wolf. All this points to the need for personalized time tools that take people into consideration.

A Flexible Resource

This book will also help you with its lack of narrow and dictatorial "shoulds" and "musts." Most of us do not need any more scoldings or "musts" about time. How most people use their time is already wrapped in strong emotions—frequently frustration and guilt. So this book does not prescribe one rigid set of rules for everyone to follow in lockstep. It does provide stimulating principles and practical ideas to help define your direction and find the tools that fit you. It does give you a foundation that rests on the reality that God is a God of order, but He doesn't spell out how to organize your sock drawer.

My work in speaking and leading seminars has taken me to many different parts of the country. I've been in touch with a wide variety of groups and individuals, including corporate directors, homemakers, counselors, pastors, church staff members, administrative people, sales people, and software engineers. Through these contacts I've come to respect the incredible time responsibilities so many people carry. And through these contacts, I have learned that many time systems fail because they assume that there is one single answer for everyone's time problems. There isn't. There is a tremendous variety of individual needs and solutions.

No one knows your pressures and problems as well as you do. That's why you are the best person to pick the tools that will work best for you.

Information and Motivation

Additionally, this book will help you with its emphasis on both information *and* motivation. Repeatedly people tell me, "I know what to do. I just don't know how to get myself to do it." Few of us consistently do all the things we know we need to be doing— whether it's exercise, eating correctly, financial planning, or spiritual growth. In situations like these, more information on time techniques isn't the solution. No amount of information will solve a motivational problem.

Finding More Time in Your Life contains dozens of practical time-improvement ideas and spells out the motivational techniques you can use to implement the ideas. In other words, it shows you how you can get yourself to do what you know you need to do—with God's wisdom and power.

> To be wise you must first have reverence for the LORD. If you know the Holy One, you have understanding. Wisdom will add years to your life (Proverbs 9:10,11 TEV).

How This Book Is Organized

To make it easy for you to find the ideas that will assist you, think of this book with one foundation and five sets of tools. The foundation is God's power and wisdom. The sets of tools are techniques and ideas to assist you in handling different challenges. Because my father was a carpenter, the image that brings me a smile is a workbench with different sets of tools hanging on Peg-Board, ready to be used on the challenge that is now on the workbench. When you have a time crunch or opportunity you want to improve, you may want to picture your own workbench with your opportunity on it, and also picture the wall nearby with your tools hanging within easy reach.

Before you look at the following tools and the principles, here's why you will also see some simple diagrams.

When E. I. DuPont first brought me into their corporation to consult and train, the executive in charge explained that they were interested in SIP—Sustained Improvements in Performance. So they funded research six weeks after each Dru Scott seminar during 12 years to see how our seminar participants improved. One conclusion the research validated was that SIP improved when we gave people memory hooks for principles and techniques. That's why this book has visual memory hooks in the chart on page 24 for each of the principles that will help you find more time in your life.

As you read about the people who are using the tools, and as you find ideas for your own situation, you may want to keep a Time Notebook. It's simply a device some people use for keeping their time insights, plans, and questions in one place. My blue binder with 8½ x 11 paper and sticky notes rests on a bookshelf near my desk and helps me keep track of ideas that bubble up. Finding more time doesn't take a lot of time, but it does take ongoing attention.

Do It Daily

In this age of flash, faithful steps in the right direction do not receive much press. However, in his bestseller, *The Tipping Point: How Little Things Can Make a Big Difference*, author Malcolm Gladwell gives renewed emphasis to how little causes can have large results.[1] Of all the people I have worked with, the ones who find the most time are the ones who know what counts and Do It Daily. They don't wait for perfect solutions. They take faithful

Quick Preview

The Strong Foundation

When you want to find more time, don't try to do it alone.

Start with God. Ask Him to be your Coach and "Wonderful Counselor." Ask for God's help, and then follow His guidance.

The Five Sets of Tools

Personality Tools—To help you know your time style so you can pick your time tools

Skip the one-size-fits-all time approaches.

Reach for the few time techniques that fit your personality, priorities, and pressures. Remember your strengths and gifts.

Focusing Tools—For direction and organization

Drop the pressure to get everything done.

Focus on the target of doing the right things at the right times.

Overcoming Tools—To gain energy and get back on the right track

Get help for straying or stalling.

Shepherd your time. Protect it, guide it, and get it back on the path and moving ahead.

Daily Tools—To gain more success with everyday time demands

Don't wait for a fix-everything, win-the-lottery solution.

Gain big improvements with daily steps in the right direction.

Spiritual Tools—To help you enjoy your Coach and Wonderful Counselor

Clean out the idea that spiritual growth is climbing a ladder to God.

Accept the gift of a loving relationship with God and grow in His love and power.

Fig. 2.1

steps in the right direction. That's why you will see this theme throughout *Finding More Time in Your Life*.

The Bible highlights the importance of Do It Daily in a special way that applies to this and any book you read. Study the Bible daily to see if what you are being taught is true.

> Now the Bereans were of more noble character than the Thessalonians, for they received the message with great eagerness and examined the Scriptures every day to see if what Paul said was true (Acts 17:11).

Protect yourself and treat yourself. Study the Bible daily to check what you are being taught. Enjoy the power of Do It Daily.

The Flip-Flop Problem

Before asking Christ Jesus to be Lord of my life, I thought everything had to be done with my power. Then for a time after trusting God, I flip-flopped to the other extreme—figuratively sitting back in a chair, hands in my lap, waiting for God to drop a picnic basket into my life with the total solution. Then reading the Bible showed me a different picture: not waiting for God to lift my feet, but walking forward while asking for His direction and power. Walking with God's power.

The Right Team

You may still be tempted to feel, "This program can't work for me. You don't know my boss, my organization, my family, my situation." Wait a moment. The fact that you are reading this book right now means your interest level is high. You don't have to do this alone. You don't have to do everything. You have God as your Wonderful Counselor and Coach. You are on a winning team. And think of the people who are finding more time. You can do it too. This is true even if those basically organized people didn't tell you all the high-value tools that are in the next chapter.

Chapter 3

What the Basically Organized People Don't Tell You

*But the wisdom that comes from heaven is first of all pure;
then peace-loving, considerate, submissive, full of mercy
and good fruit, impartial and sincere.*

James 3:17

What's Ahead

- Two major ways of handling time and how it helps to know which one relates to you.
- The 19 things basically organized people do but don't talk about.
- How to get help from a basically organized person.

Many people feel that everyone else in the world is on top of their time and has everything focused, organized, and scheduled. This is not true.

When I speak at conventions and conferences, I often take a quick poll. First, I explain what I call Category One (basically orderly) and Category Two (needs to concentrate to be orderly). Then, I ask the people in the audience to raise their hands to show how they rate themselves.

When I ask Category One people to raise their hands, a few hands go up across the auditorium. When I ask how many are like me, and rate themselves as a Category Two, more than 70 percent of the people consistently raise their hands. When people look around you can hear the laughs of surprise to discover how many are Category Twos.

You can also hear laughter when I ask the Category One people in the audience if they are married to a Category Two. So even if you are basically orderly, you probably have some of us in your life. Even if you are a part of the minority, you will find these Category Two tools both useful and helpful to understand. Here's why. The majority of people claim a Category Two rating in at least one area of their lives. Maybe at home. Maybe in relationships. Maybe in finances.

If you are not sure if you are a Category One or Two with your time, you are probably a Category One. Category Twos know who they are.

Category Two, need-to-concentrate-to-be-organized people are encouraged when they realize that although most time books are written for Category One people—who are basically organized—there are more Category Two people. We are not alone. We are actually the majority. This information explains why so many people have read a time book and said, "But my situation is different." Improvements call for a special set of tools when you are a Category Two. Let me explain in more detail.

Category One people write lists and scratch off items. They have all their Christmas shopping done and wrapped in September. They have all their tax records and receipts in files. They start their taxes on New Year's Day as they munch on chips and dip and watch football games on TV.

Category Two people are different. They write lists but lose some of them. The day before they want to hand someone a Christmas gift, they squeeze through the crowds in the stores. Right after the holidays and during the games on New Year's Day, they might think about their tax returns, but probably not for long. And they still end up getting an IRS extension or driving to the post office on April 15.

By the way, if you were to drive to the main post office in San Francisco on April 15 at 11 P.M., you would be greeted by hundreds of people in cars, men and women on sidewalks cheering and waving, musicians playing, and merchants handing out free ice cream. It's a block party for crowds of Category Two people.

Why It's Important to Know Which Category You Are

When you know which category you tilt toward, you know which time tools to use. The Category One person will find value in traditional time tools. The Category Two person benefits by traditional tools plus adding the tailored tools that relate to his or her personality, pressures, and priorities.

It's also interesting to remember that because a Category One will usually marry a Category Two, and will often work with a Category Two, this information helps naturally organized people in terms of providing the right amount of support and the right amount of self-protection.

Understanding Category One or Two differences also helps the basically organized person to be more tolerant. It's easy for a Category One to stand up and ask, "Why don't you just get your act together?" With increased understanding, it is easier for a Category One to be thankful for what he or she has naturally and also to be more patient with what the Twos are concentrating on acquiring. (A word of warning. It's not fair for a Category Two to throw his hands up in the air and demand rights with, "You can't expect more. I'm a Category Two.")

Understanding your tendency helps you focus on what is important for you. The Category Two needs to focus on tools that the Category One person may not need. For example, we've all heard that we need to plan. We've heard that five minutes of planning will save 50 minutes of doing. We've heard that five minutes of planning can save a special trip to the store for one needed item. We've heard that five minutes of planning can help you get everything accomplished in one meeting and erase the need for follow-up phone calls or additional meetings.

However, we've rarely heard that if you are a Category Two, you will benefit by doing more planning in writing than your Category One colleague needs. While the Category One might do his planning in his mind as he walks up the stairs on his way to work, the Category Two benefits by sitting down earlier with pencil, notes, and calendar in hand and writing what he wants to accomplish the next year, the next week, and the next day. Category Twos thrive on having written weekly and daily targets.

Because Category Ones and Twos do things differently, more understanding helps clean out the conflict and increases respect and cooperation.

"I Can't Stand Her. She's So Organized."

Because most of my consulting and training in corporations has centered on repeat business and customer satisfaction, this has allowed me to get to know a number of Category One people without them thinking of me as a time person. (When people see you as an expert on time and organization, you are not popular. People try to cover their desks. They say, "It doesn't usually look like this." Or they apologize for a stack of papers.) However, because I am a time person at heart, finding better ways to use time is always at the back of my mind no matter what the project. So sometimes when I see someone doing something well, I'll ask them to tell me more about how they do it.

For example, I was in the office of a manager with over 2,000 people in his organization and his desk had three things on it with a computer on his credenza. Other managers in the same organization had papers piled everywhere. When I asked him how he handled paperwork so well, he looked blank, and then replied, "I get rid of it right away. It's just common sense."

Here's another example. I was in the garage of a friend who homeschools five children and who is married to a man who could wear a T-shirt with "I'm a Category Two" printed on the front. Their garage was so neat and orderly you could have given a party in it. When I asked her how she did it, she gave the classic answer of a basically organized Category One: "Keep it clean I suppose. I just use common sense."

So here's the secret: If you have an area where you struggle, find a Category One who is good in that area and watch them. Asking them how they do it usually produces little. They often don't know how they do it and then throw out that answer of "just common sense." So watch the people who star in an area of your development. Put on a Sherlock Holmes detective hat and sleuth how they do it. It's fun to watch a star and learn from someone who does something well.

The Tools Category One People Use

During the years of watching people who are Category Ones, I have collected a list of the tools they frequently use. Although many of these are covered in detail later in the book, here is a quick overview.

Because some Category Two people start to sweat when they see a list with 19 items, think of these ideas as tools hanging on a Peg-Board wall. No one uses all of them. As you look at the list, pick one tool that will bring relief and make a difference for you today. (You can always come back later and choose a different tool.)

1. Allow time in and time out

"Work hard and play hard" may be the motto. Or it may be "Sunday is a day of rest." Consistently effective people turn off the switch, put their feet up, and have deliberate time for relaxation.

2. Anticipate and prevent problems

Think ahead and prepare for what might go wrong. Twos are often surprised when they encounter problems. Category Ones anticipate and prevent.

3. Avoid searching by having no temporary parking places

Imagine a sign next to your phone that says: No temporary parking places. Put it in place or in use. When you acquire something, immediately assign it a regular parking place. Many people can find an hour a week with this one tool. So when you put the phone back in the cradle, remind yourself, "In use or in place. No temporary parking places."

4. Carry and use a daily action sheet of some kind

Whether it's a Palm Pilot, a 3 x 5 card in your pocket, a page with yellow sticky notes next to your calendar, or a list on the refrigerator, Category Ones have a written daily focus in hand, and they have a written weekly focus within reach. Although several highly successful Category Ones I have interviewed do not have written objectives, most do. And most have them close at hand.

5. Celebrate

Whether it is kneeling and giving thanks, patting yourself on the back, or drawing a red line through an accomplishment listed on your daily action sheet—or all of the above—take the time to celebrate. It feels good. It puts gas in your tank. And it moves you ahead.

6. Divide big jobs into workable steps

You can take on a job as big as a football field and get it done by cutting it into ten-yard pieces. When you divide big jobs into steps you help yourself concentrate. You motivate yourself. You free yourself to accomplish one step at a time.

7. Do central and essential priorities now

Doing the Central Priorities now—the important but not urgent things like taking care of your spiritual life, your physical fitness, and your financial future—prevents big problems later on. And doing your Essential Priorities now—the important and urgent things like a report that is due this afternoon or a phone call that needs to be made—prevents problems that could disrupt your life today. The secret is not just do them first; it is do them now.

8. Do it daily

People who give, receive, and enjoy the most are the ones who are taking care of things daily. They don't just concentrate before the end of the quarter or before company comes to visit. Daily faithful steps in the right direction beat occasional flashes of productivity.

9. Enjoy giving

This biblical paradox is true. There is more happiness in giving than in receiving. The people who have the most energy for accomplishments and lifestyle are the ones who invest time volunteering for things like teaching English as a second language, visiting a convalescent hospital, or teaching a Bible study. The pathway to happiness and energy is giving and serving.

10. Finish fully

Complete as much as you can. Write the email, attach the document, and send it. This is a small example of finishing fully. Make the bed. Take a shower and get completely dressed first thing in the morning. Plan a meeting, hold it, and end it by writing down next steps. Take a task to completion and get joy from crossing the finish line. I love the picture of a race with the runner crossing the finish line and breaking the ribbon across her chest. Finish fully.

Picking One Tool at a Time

If you are a Category Two at this midpoint in the list, it may be tempting to feel guilty or depressed, but don't do it. Again, picture a worktable with all the tools hanging on a Peg-Board. Then remind yourself, you only need to reach for the one that will help you now. And that tool may be the next one in this collection of what Category One people do.

11. Group-related activities

If you have ever made a trip to a grocery store for one missing ingredient, you know the importance of grouping related items. So while you are out shopping, group all the needed items and all the other errands. If you are writing letters, group a couple more. It is almost as easy to write three as one. When you are buying a birthday card, buy all the cards for the month at the same time.

12. Help others get what they want

Adding this dimension benefits you two ways. It keeps you focused on others by constantly asking yourself, "What do they want?" And it gives you the joy of assisting them. Often it only takes a phone call, an introduction, an article, or a book. Help others get what they want and you help yourself have more energy and joy.

13. Plan frequently

When Kelly, a magna cum laude bachelor's degree graduate and now part of a fast-track management program, was asked when she planned, she replied instantly, "I plan all the time." At a meeting in Los Angeles, I had the opportunity to sit next to management guru Peter F. Drucker just before he spoke, and even though his presentation was later in the program, he was already planning when it would end, how long the drive back to his Claremont home would take, and when he could swim before he taught a class that night. I suspect he plans all the time too.

Planning prevents problems. Planning shows you where you can contribute to your objectives. Planning pays off for you and others. While Category Ones plan all the time, Category Twos move farther with planning regularly.

14. Put a cushion in your calendar

This alliterative phrase can help you remember how comfortable it can be if you allow some emergency time before a deadline. As soon as a big project or trip is scheduled, one very effective Category One woman I know opens her calendar and writes in "Emergency Day" on one or two days before the due date. She schedules these weeks in advance as a cushion she works diligently not to need. One Category One man says he gets completely dressed a full hour before he leaves home for a meeting. Give yourself a cushion.

15. Set and meet deadlines

Deadlines energize and stimulate. They help you enjoy getting things done that would otherwise slide.

16. Standardize and simplify

Here are some quick examples that show the benefits of standardizing and simplifying. One man saves time in the morning by standardizing his work clothes. He wears only variations of khaki pants and denim shirts. One teacher of a women's Bible study standardizes her giving. When she finds a book she enjoys, she buys it by the stack. Simplifying helps her give gifts that are always the right size, the right color, and fit well in any style décor. One mother standardizes and simplifies her menu planning by "fixing faces for dinner" on Wednesday nights when her husband works late and she and the children eat together. She spreads each plate with cottage cheese and puts a tray of veggies, olives for eyes, and strips of cold cuts on the table. All the children try to make the wildest and best faces on the plate full of cottage cheese before they applaud each face and are "allowed" to eat anything.

17. Track your time

Category Ones keep track of their time. They know how long it takes to do everything, and that helps them schedule and know when they are improving. This tool helps others with their time too. The first time I held a customizing interview with the head of a large research center, I actually finished the interview, but because it was the end of the day, I kept sitting and chatting a bit. Never again. Before we stood to shake hands goodbye, he looked at his watch, tapped its stopwatch function, and noted, "An hour and seven minutes."

18. Use timetables

Timetables increase your productivity at the start of a project. They help you relax because you know when you are on schedule. And they soften the pressure at the end because you have completed so many steps.

19. Work in cycles

When you finish something, start preparing for the next event. As Shannon is putting her two young children to bed, she tosses their dirty clothes into the hamper and lays out their clothes for the next morning. As Bert leaves the barbershop, he looks at his new haircut in the mirror and makes an appointment for his next haircut. As Millie finishes putting her Christmas decorations away, she starts thinking about the people she loves. Then she sits at her desk, begins her Christmas-gift list, and starts her year-long fun of finding and making the perfect gifts.

As you consider this collection of Category One tools, you may want to pick one you can use now, or you may treat the collection as a reference you can reach for in the future. Whichever you do, you will have more fun watching the people who star in the areas you want to develop.

Special Notes for Category Two People

1. Be kind to Category Ones. Never make fun of them. Skip saying things like, "He's so organized, I can't stand it." Treat them with respect. They are your friends, and your life is easier for being around them. (And their lives are more exciting for being around you!)

2. Barter with Category Ones. If Ones will let you watch and work with them, polish their shoes. Not really, but be willing to do some work they don't want to do. Don't be a drain or a taker. You have much to gain by watching and learning from them because you can learn to do it too.

3. Don't count on a Category One to help you pick your organizer. They don't talk about organizers and calendars very much for two reasons. They have one that is working well for them, so why mention it? The second reason is they often don't need much of a system.

On the other hand, if you are a Category Two, you will hang on to your organizer like a life ring in a stormy sea. When an earthquake hit the San Francisco area, I grabbed my organizer as I fled my office. I later learned that earthquake experts tell you to leave the organizer and take cover where you are. While you don't need an organizer in an earthquake, it does help in many other areas.

The Right Motivation

While calendars and organizers help bring order to both Category One and Two people, I like to tuck a 3 x 5 card in my calendar with a quote to remind me of the source of the "what" I most long for. The source is not the organizer or even the order it helps produce. The source is not right priorities or even right tools. The ultimate source is God's Spirit, who works in our lives in many ways.

> But the Spirit produces love, joy, peace, patience, kindness, goodness, faithfulness, humility, and self-control (Galatians 5:22,23 TEV).

I find it comforting to realize that even if someone is a Category One in time, he or she may be a Category Two in relationships or in finances. We all have different gifts and different strengths. The bottom line is that we need each other. Believe that we can all grow and improve. And pick the tools that relate to you—particularly the ones that help erase any of the dangerous myths in the next chapter.

Part II

Personality
Tools

*For Knowing Yourself
and Picking Your Tools*

PERSONALITY TOOLS

FOR KNOWING YOURSELF AND PICKING YOUR TOOLS

❧ Skip the one-size-fits-all time approaches.

❧ Reach for the few time techniques that fit your personality, priorities, and pressures. Remember your strengths and gifts.

Chapter 4

Exposing the Myths About Time Success

He stores up wisdom for those who are honest.
Proverbs 2:7 NCV

What's Ahead

• Ten myths that can steal your time.
• The amazing things you can accomplish in only 15 minutes a day.

Start with God and you gain understanding. God's truth is not only a time-saver, it gives you the ability to see yourself and your situation with new eyes, with new honesty, and with new hope. Feel the hope you have when you find practical time tools that are right for your personality. And feel the hope you have when you are using the tools that fit your strengths and gifted areas. This combination of tools for your strengths and gifts will bring relief and make a major difference in your life. For example, the powerful Grab 15 tool at the end of this chapter may be the one that is exactly what you have been wanting.

Many of us struggle in being successful with our time because we unknowingly distract ourselves with inaccurate assumptions. These assumptions are so common that many accept them without ever questioning their validity. However, as you examine them, you will see what they are: mere myths that can distract you from picking the right tools for your personality, your pressures, and your priorities.

The Ten Most Common Myths About Time Success

1. "But there's nothing I can do."

If you find yourself making this statement, you may be reacting to a pressure-packed situation. It may describe your feelings of being overwhelmed, but it's not an accurate statement of your time capabilities. You may not always be able to do everything you would like to do or need to do, but you can certainly take some steps. A small step in the right direction is much better than waiting until you can do everything.

For example, you may need a full eight hours to write a tough report, but that block of time simply may not be available. Don't let that stop you from taking some action. Carve out a half hour each day to work on the report. It's not ideal, but it adds up and it will help. At the very least, this approach will allay those feelings of being swamped and put you back on track in the situation. Remind yourself: "I always have choices. There's always something I can do." This bit of truth will turn problems into opportunities.

2. "It doesn't work for me."

If you've made this statement in the past, take a minute to examine how you use this expression. It's accurate to say that some time techniques may not meet your needs. If this is the case, put those techniques aside and select others that do.

If, on the other hand, this statement conveys a hidden hope that the technique alone will do the job for you, reconsider. A workbench full of tools is useless without a pair of hands to do the work. Time techniques are only tools; they can help make our work easier, but they can't do the job by themselves. Their degree of usefulness depends on the skill with which we use them. We sharpen our skills when we use them again and again. They are most beneficial when we integrate them into our daily activities.

Select your time techniques wisely. Experiment to find the ones that work best for you. Develop your skill in using them. Put them to work for you on an ongoing basis. It's a matter of picking the right tools and using them. The tools alone won't do it, but you can do it with their help.

3. "I always lose my list."

Most of us don't realize how complex we are. Our needs and desires are often in flux, and sometimes actually in direct opposition to each other. Everyone has mixed feelings at one time or another. Part of a person may sincerely, even desperately, want to use time more effectively. Another facet of that same person may fear the change that smoother operation could bring. As soon as that person has written a well-intentioned to-do list, another facet accidentally tucks it into some out-of-the-way corner. This isn't schizophrenic. It simply reveals how complex and intricate we all are. Conflicting feelings are common human behavior.

Betsy, a habitual list-loser, found a creative way to solve her problem. "Accepting that I both loved and hated my 'Must Do' lists gave me an entirely new perspective," she told me. "I wanted to get things done, but every time I saw those words, 'Must Do,' at the top of my daily list, I felt nagged. I was always losing my list, scolding myself for losing it, taking more time to write out another list—and then losing that one too! I solved my problem when I changed the title of the list. Now I write a list of 'Potential Accomplishments' each day and hang it right by the telephone. I haven't lost one since," she concluded with a smile.

Although list-losing may be one of your time problems, Betsy's particular solution may not be the best one for you. The important thing to remember is that we all have mixed feelings. Recognize them and accept them as part of the human condition. If you lose lists continually, analyze your feelings and find out why. Work out a creative solution acceptable to all the facets of your own personality.

4. "But I've already taken the course or read the book."

"The rich get richer" is an old saying, but it still applies. Something that used to surprise me about the organizations that bring me in to help them with customer satisfaction and repeat business is that they are already doing well. Then I learned that the best cooks buy cookbooks. People who play the best golf buy golf videos. Artistic people buy books on decorating. And people who do well with their time buy books on time and are given books on time.

You have never eaten a meal so nourishing that you don't have to eat again. You have to refill the gas tank periodically if you want to keep driving your car. Just as there are no one-time meals or always-full gas tanks, there are no one-time courses or books. So getting organized and using your time well is not a "once only" get-organized project, it's an ongoing program to bring the order you want into your life.

Read books. Take courses. Listen to tapes. And talk with people. Keep yourself well supplied with ideas and inspiration. It's one of the best ways to keep yourself on target with your time.

5. "I just can't get organized around here."

There's no question about it—it is easier to get organized when the people around you use their time well. That's one reason why it pays off to help others improve their use of time. But don't let an imperfect situation be an excuse to do nothing about your own time problems. Resentment about the disorganization around you is a waste of your time. Take the initiative. Work on improving your own time use. Do what you can, regardless of less-than-ideal circumstances.

Let the people around you know you are working to improve your time use. Respect the fact that some of them have rough situations. Some may not believe that time skills can make a difference. Don't focus on their disorganization. Instead, ask them how you can make your time together more productive. Your questions may help them see their own time problems in a new light and provide an inspiring model. Even if you can't produce an ideal situation, you will be getting more from your own time. That alone can lead to an appreciable improvement in your situation.

6. "I can't get organized because people keep interrupting me."

For most of us, interruptions are a problem. We may long to lock ourselves safely away from all distractions, but we rarely achieve that blissful state. Waiting for it to materialize before you begin to get a better handle on your time is as fruitless as waiting for that mythical 25-hour day. Interruptions are an inevitable part of everyday living. Don't waste time waiting for them to disappear. Learn how to handle them instead. It's vital to successful time management.

Other chapters will show you how to get what you want and need from your time in spite of interruptions. You can learn how to deal with interrupters courteously, considerately, and creatively. Whether you have two toddlers underfoot or an office full of talkative coworkers, you can learn techniques that will free you from many unnecessary interruptions.

7. "Time management is boring."

Traditional time management can be boring. And most of us aren't willing to suffer the boredom even though we really do want to be more productive. Those last-minute rushes are exciting, and there can be an intense thrill in handling a crisis. We may pay a high price for this excitement, but at least we're not bored.

If you have not explored time techniques because they are boring, I have good news. You can use your time skillfully and still keep it as stimulating and exciting as you want it to be. Making time management effective and exciting is the revolutionary thrust of this book.

8. "I'll get so organized I won't get anything done."

There's often a hidden fear behind this concern—the fear that someone or something will control you. Therefore, it is crucial to understand that time techniques cannot control you. You are in charge of them. They are only a passive collection of tools that you can use in any way you wish. You are the one who is in control of your time.

If you express this concern, I know that you are already aware of the danger of becoming a "list and schedule fanatic"— someone who makes dozens of lists but gets nothing done. You don't have to worry. If you are reading this book, you are not the kind of person who would spend so much time getting organized that you couldn't get anything accomplished.

9. "I need someone to motivate me."

This myth is based on the common belief that someone or something outside ourselves controls our feelings. The idea crops up in hundreds of common expressions: "You make me angry" and "You make me happy" are two prime examples. Although they are common, they aren't accurate. We may feel angry about a particular incident or a colleague's behavior, but that person or event does not have the power to make us angry. We may feel happy when we hear a lovely song or see someone we admire, but that song or person doesn't make us happy. It's a fine distinction, but an important one. The reality is that we are all in charge of our own feelings. The language in this book was carefully selected to reinforce that reality. You won't read that anger sets up a barrier to good time management. You will read that you may delay solving time problems when you are angry. You are in charge of your own feelings. You don't have to wait for anyone else to inspire you. You can become your own inspiration.

10. "I'm waiting until I have more time."

This is a very common myth. Consider it logically and you'll realize it doesn't hold up. Putting off doing what counts most to you now until you have "more time" is like saying you can't go on a diet until you lose some weight.

Many of us let ourselves slide into believing that someday when the kids grow up, when the mortgage is paid off, when we have a better job, when a new relationship develops, something different will happen. Suddenly we'll have more time to do what we want or need to do. This passive "waiting until" attitude allows precious time to slip through our fingers like water, to disappear forever.

"I'm waiting until I have more time" is not an accurate statement of reality. It's an outmoded state of mind. A colleague of mine realized this one day when she visited her 81-year-old aunt in a retirement home. It was just two days before Christmas, and my friend was caught up in her usual last-minute holiday rush. As she drove up the road to the retirement community, she reflected that one benefit of retirement would be a greater amount of free time to do the things she felt her busy life now kept her from doing.

The scene at the retirement center put an end to that myth. Five residents waited impatiently in the hall for a minibus that would take them to town for some last-minute errands. A woman went whizzing by in her motorized wheelchair, muttering that she'd never get all her cards in the mail on time. A member of the decoration committee was explaining that she hadn't had time to order the new lights. To cap it all, my colleague's aunt came breathlessly to meet her, upset that she still hadn't finished making all her gifts for the family.

At that moment, my friend realized that no matter how long she waited, she'd never have that mythical state of "more time" dropped in her lap.

Accept the reality of the 24-hour day. Rather than investing your energies in futile waiting "until," you can get the most out of this moment. You can decide, and you can do it.

Clear Out the Waiting Myth and Grab 15

To prove that these myths can be replaced with something better, use the Grab 15 tool to replace the waiting-until myth. The Grab 15 tool means picking a project that has been gathering the dust of delay and spending 15 minutes on it each day.

You will be amazed at what you can accomplish by using this tool. Here's my trophy example. When I couldn't get my car into a stuffed garage, using the Grab 15 tool enabled me to drive that car in before four weeks had rolled by.

For most people the hardest part of a big job is getting started. When you promise yourself that your commitment is for only 15 minutes, it's much easier to begin. For some, Grab 15 might mean to find some way, small or large, to simplify your life each day.

Consider what you can accomplish by consistently investing 15 minutes a day:

- Write a manual
- Remodel a room
- Catch up on financial paperwork
- Grow a small garden
- Flatten your stomach
- Learn a new language in three years
- Read the entire Bible in a year
- Learn a new computer application
- Learn to read financial reports

A Remodeled Bathroom with Grab 15

Author Charlotte Hale Allen saw tangible proof of this powerful technique when she and her husband visited a friend in a small Southern town. Their friend was the town's only doctor and the new owner of a rambling house that had been vacant for years. When they arrived, their friend was standing in the middle of a room with paint cans and tools scattered across the floor. He looked at the high ceiling and declared, "That has got to come down." They thought he was merely dreaming until he took them into his new bathroom. The ceiling was lowered. New cabinets were installed. New plumbing was in place. He smiled as he pointed with pride to the heated towel bar he had installed.

When they asked how he did it, he smiled again and said, "It's simple. I work at least 15 minutes a day, every day, without fail."

Grab 15 and Gain 78 Hours

Here are the specifics: 15 minutes a day equals 78 hours a year. Fifteen minutes a day, day after day, quickly adds up. Even if you take Sunday off, you can chalk up 90 productive minutes a week. Just look at the proof:

15 minutes x 6 days = 90 minutes a week

90 minutes a week x 52 = 4,680 minutes, which equals 78 hours!

Imagine what you could accomplish if someone waved a wand and magically gave you 78 extra hours! The Grab 15 technique puts that magic wand in your own hands! Here are some of the added benefits of the Grab 15 technique.

Enjoy the creativity benefit of Grab 15. When you work on a task for 15 minutes a day, that task is always simmering on the back burner of your mind. And your creativity is simmering when you commit to Grab 15. Even when you are not consciously thinking about the job, your subconscious is working for you.

Enjoy the bonus benefit of Grab 15. Some days, after you finish your 15-minute commitment, you'll be on a roll. You'll feel like continuing. And you will. That bonus effort will bring you that much closer to your goal.

Here is a variation on Grab 15 that scored high votes from a group who were all earning over $250,000 a year. This tool is: Grab 15 minutes a day for your self-development.

That morning, the conference room and the crystal chandelier at the Ritz-Carlton had a special sparkle for me as I stood in the back of the room talking to the people who had heard my presentation. In it, we had explored a number of ideas to build your success with time.

At the end of the session, in a quick survey of the 120 people, I asked them to write down which one idea was the most valuable for them. There was no contest. The poll rated one idea the highest: Grab 15 minutes a day—without fail—for studying for your self-development.

The Grab 15 tool can clear out the waiting-until myth and many other tired assumptions.

Clear Out All the Old Myths— Give Yourself a Fresh Start

If any of the above myths sound familiar, keep your ears open. When you hear yourself or someone else make one of these statements, remember what you've learned in this chapter:

- Myths are nothing more than stumbling blocks. Don't allow them to block you from experiencing the richness of each moment.

- Replace the myths with the time tools that fit your personality, your pressures, and your priorities.

Free yourself to find more time in spite of the secret pleasures of misusing time.

Chapter 5

The Secret Pleasures of Mismanaging Time

A tranquil heart is life to the body.

Proverbs 14:30 NASB

What's Ahead

- *A new look at some old problems.*
- *How some persistent problems may be paying rewards under the table.*

You may be all too familiar with the problems that misusing time can stir up. But did you ever realize that misusing time offers secret pleasures as well? Without being aware of it, you may already have a clue as to what they are. You may have even experienced some of them yourself. Persistent problems often signal secret pleasures.

Have you ever put off an important project until the last minute—even when you could have done it earlier? Ever made a wild and frantic dash to get to an appointment you could have left for sooner? Have you ever known an activity was off target and heading you straight for a time crunch—and you still kept at it? Those last-minute crunches are charged with electricity, aren't they?

Mismanaging time can pay off in some rarely revealed ways that many of us unknowingly take advantage of. Some of us mismanage time to get attention or gain a sense of power. Mismanaging time also can serve as a way to avoid unpleasant tasks or shirk personal responsibility. It can be used to resist change, sidestep new feelings, avoid feeling close to others, and deal with that age-old fear of feeling "too good."

However, don't make a blanket indictment of the time practices this chapter will reveal. We all gain something from our use of time even when we mismanage it. And it is helpful to understand what those secret payoffs are. When you understand motivations, you work more effectively with the people around you. Most of all, you work more effectively with yourself. You don't have to change your behavior just because you've learned about these secret payoffs, but if you decide you want to, you can do it faster and more easily.

Six Secret Pleasures of Time Mismanagement

1. Getting attention—"Look, ma, no hands!"

In today's crowded, rushed, and anonymous world, it's hard to dream up any surefire techniques for being noticed. Time misuse has emerged as one of the few proven attention-getters.

Picture the people in your life who don't handle their time well. It's highly probable that this behavior gets them a lot of attention. Relatives nag them, coworkers chide them, friends schedule plans around them. People kid them about it. Sometimes the attention leaves a bad taste in their mouths; it's not always complimentary or admiring. But it is attention. Mismanaging their time gets them noticed.

Loretta makes herself the center of attention at staff meetings—regularly scheduled meetings, special project meetings, even emergency meetings. She arrives late, bursting in with breathless apologies. She drops a load of charts and notes on the table and pushes past everyone to get to the coatrack in the back of the room. She rattles the metal coat hangers, apologizing again for the interruption. Then she offers a string of loudly whispered "excuse me's" as she wriggles through the group to get to her seat. Although the other staff members are familiar with her antics, she is always noticed. She captures everyone's attention—and their time.

The late-arrival technique has many variations, but it's always an attention-getter. Surely you've run into someone who arrives late at every party and makes a "grand entrance." What about the dinner guest who is chronically late? All the other guests have been there for an hour. They've munched through the hors d'oeuvres and made inroads on the salted peanuts. They want to sit down to dinner. Delicious aromas waft from the kitchen, and the hostess is beginning to worry that the veal will be over-cooked. The host wonders what he should do. Then in sails the latecomer, full of excuses. Everyone is so happy they can finally eat that, instead of being greeted angrily, he or she is welcomed with relief.

Arriving late is an old and common way to get attention. Those who make it a practice may be reluctant to give it up until they find something that works just as well. In subsequent chapters, you'll discover a variety of ways that such people can learn to get the recognition they want and deserve without imposing unfairly on others.

2. Secret power—"I'll show you who's boss."

Many people feel powerless to control their own destiny in our modern mass society. Some react by trying to gain control in a variety of everyday situations. For example, on her way out to lunch with a group of friends, Mindy decides that she must redo her makeup. The others shift around in the hall waiting for her, looking at their watches and calculating whether they will get to the restaurant on time. Mindy gains control by making them wait and controlling when they leave.

A major aspect of control is determining "when." If the information systems department delays the start of a marketing campaign because forecasts are late, information systems is in control. If a subordinate holds up the new project plans because he hasn't finished the graphics, unconsciously he is showing everyone who's boss. He also may risk planting the suspicion that he's inefficient, but for the moment, he gains a sense of control. If a low-ranking civilian guard on a military base stops every entering vehicle to make a maddeningly meticulous examination of passes, he's in control. A long line of colonels and captains may fume as they sit in their cars at the gate to the military base, but the guard controls the slow-moving line. This kind of control may only offer a false sense of power, but it is one of the ways mismanaging time can pay off.

3. Sidestepping the unpleasant—"I'm too busy to take out the garbage."

Another reward of mismanaged time is the excuse to avoid some unpleasant duty. A personnel director of a company told me, "I know that a section manager needs to talk to one of his employees about her body odor. Customers even mention it. Whenever I ask him about it, he always tells me that he knows it's important but he hasn't had time. He's been putting off this unpleasant chore for months because he's been 'running behind.'"

One dedicated volunteer in our community hates housework. She keeps so busy raising funds for charities and canvassing the neighborhood for political campaigns that she has no time to attack the muddy paw prints on the carpet or the grime in the bathroom.

A father who works extremely long hours may feel totally justified in doing no housework, ignoring the dirty storm drains, or refusing to face the reality that one of his teenage children has a potential drug problem.

If everyone in the group knows that Jim never catches up on his workload, he won't receive extra responsibilities. When a difficult project comes up, it's given to someone else.

Running behind is a common excuse for putting off something that is hard to face. People even use it to avoid doing anything unpleasant at all.

4. Avoiding new feelings—"Don't rock the boat."

Mismanaging time is an effective way to avoid certain emotions or self-evaluations. The emotions may be painful feelings of rejection, awkwardness, or failure; they can also be pleasant feelings of acceptance and love for who we are, intimacy with someone we love, or success. Although it is hard to believe that someone would want to avoid such emotions, the unfamiliar can often be frightening.

A hardworking young executive assistant constantly talks about taking a class on salsa dancing at the local community college to expand her social life. Each term, however, she's "just too busy" to sign up. Unconsciously, she's afraid she'll feel awkward or clumsy when she's learning the dance steps, or she's nervous about opening conversations with strangers. So she spends her evenings reading instead of making the new friends she wants.

A college professor puts off completing his novel. He's too busy making lesson plans. Although he's not aware of it, he fears becoming a successful novelist. His parents were working-class people who never completed high school. The status of a college professor is a dizzying one by comparison. If he were to become a celebrated novelist on top of that, he is afraid he might be in over his head. The lesson plans get written—the novel doesn't.

Sales people who procrastinate and develop "call reluctance" are often fending off feelings of rejection. If you want to ask someone out to dinner but keep putting it off, it could be for the same reason. You might have an enjoyable date, but you don't want to risk being turned down.

Some people feel that their work is the only justification for their existence. They hide themselves in busywork because they fear the unfamiliar feelings of being loved and accepted for who they are, not just for what they do.

Most of us have mixed emotions about new situations and new feelings. A part of us may desperately want to feel successful, loved, accepted, and positive about ourselves and our lives. Another part may find it's not always easy to embrace new feelings. It can be difficult to let go of the familiar, even when it's painful.

5. Shirking personal responsibility—"Why didn't you remind me?"

Time misuse can serve as a handy excuse for sidestepping personal responsibility.

A teenager misses his appointment at the orthodontist and blusters to his mother, "You're supposed to keep track of dates. Why didn't you remind me?"

A defensive husband wails to his wife, "You know I wanted to get you an anniversary present. Why didn't you tell me it was today?"

A woman driving her children to a mountain campsite fumes when they run out of gas on a lonely road, "I can't keep my eyes on the gas gauge when I'm driving. Why didn't you remind me to get gas in that last town?"

Some people continually mismanage their time to avoid accepting responsibility. They want somebody else to do the job for them.

Sandy blithely tells everyone that she never wears a watch. "There are plenty of watches around here." She's really saying, "It's your responsibility to make sure I get where I'm going on time."

Tossing responsibility to someone else isn't a payoff that many people are aware they get from mismanaging their time. Keep your ears open, though. You'll be surprised at how often you hear some variety of, "Why didn't you remind me?"

6. Resisting change—"I've always done it this way."

People resist change largely because familiar ways of doing things have become comfortable habits. They are like the big, old, comfortable armchair a friend's grandfather refused to give up. The upholstery was faded. The stuffing was showing through some of the cushions. And some of the springs were useless, but he refused to get a new chair.

"That old chair is comfortable," he affirmed stoutly. "Sitting in something new to read the paper wouldn't seem natural."

If time misuse has become a comfortable old habit, it, too, will feel "natural." You may resist a more pleasurable and productive method because it feels strange and unnatural at first. You may hang on to the old habit even if it is no longer useful.

A manager who once did all her inputting at the computer has this problem. When her assistant produces a document with mistakes, she fixes it herself. "It saves time," she says. In the long run it would save more time to teach her assistant how to be accurate.

Fear of Feeling "Too Good"

Many people mismanage their time because of a fear that's as old as history. It's the illogical but very common feeling that if things are going too smoothly, fate will intervene. Something bad is bound to happen. They don't want to risk that, so they mismanage their time—it's a kind of hex-insurance.

Many of us also have absorbed the concept that there's something wrong about enjoyment. If we have too much fun, punishment lurks around the corner. If it feels good, then it must be either fattening, sinful, or carcinogenic.

When you invest your time well, you feel good and enjoy life more. If you're afraid of feeling too good, you have a classic reason to avoid putting your life in order. You gain too much from your inefficient use of time.

Forestalling the possibility of feeling too good may seem like a negative payoff, but it is one of the most common reasons why people don't use their time skillfully. You can overcome this outdated fear. God invented joy.

Avoiding Closeness

Another deep-seated reason for the mismanagement of time is the fear of closeness. Unknowingly, we may set ourselves up to avoid the opportunity for intimacy—even with those we love.

One business man literally built a wall between himself and his wife with his laptop computer. As she sat across from him at the table after dinner, he'd flip through folders with one hand and tap in sales figures with the other. She saw more of his laptop than she did of him. There was no opportunity for intimate conversation.

A recently divorced woman confessed that she now realized she had used an endless supply of chores like armor. She never had time to talk with her husband about his problems. When she did listen, she was always attending to something else—cataloging the slides from last year's vacation, sorting the children's laundry, balancing the checkbook. She said her marriage didn't explode all at once. It just slowly came apart at the seams.

Even in the act of seeking closeness, some of us find ways to avoid it. Consider the dating couple who plan an intimate evening of a concert and dining. Neither makes a reservation at a restaurant. They spend their first 20 minutes deciding where to eat, then another ten minutes trying to book a table. When they are finally seated, they are hungry and irritable. There's no time left to savor the food. They must bolt it down if they are to get to the concert by curtain time. They lose the pleasure of a good dinner and each other's company. Then they dash to the concert and sit through the program feeling anything but close.

In conclusion, be aware of ways to mismanage time, but keep in mind a word of caution. Do not walk up to someone in your life and say, "You're just putting this off to avoid feeling too good." You won't help people, and you may lose your friends by labeling them. So don't announce your speculations about someone else unless they ask for your insights. People signal their readiness to hear advice by asking for it. This is a lesson I'm still learning.

The Secret Is Out, but Must You Change?

- You don't necessarily have to change your behavior. You can go right on making those late-arrival "grand entrances" at parties if you want to. It's your choice.

- We all use our time to get something. It may be what we feel we need at the moment, or it may be something we needed in the past. Understand what it is. Face up to mixed feelings in yourself and others.

- When you understand conflicting motivations, you don't have to change anything. But this knowledge helps you make changes if that's what you decide to do.

- Change requires courage and determination. It holds the threat as well as the thrill of the unknown. When Shakespeare's Hamlet observes that we prefer to "bear those ills we have than fly to others that we know not of," he sums things up more poetically than a psychology textbook, but the idea is the same.

- Don't give up old ways of mismanaging time until you are ready to risk the rewards of greeting life with open arms, willing to accept the challenge, growth, and richness it offers.

Chapter 6

Your Stimulation and Excitement Quota and Your Time

Above all else, guard your heart, for it is the wellspring of life.
Proverbs 4:23

What's Ahead

- *What's behind last-minute rushes.*
- *What happens to your time when you don't put the right amount of excitement in your calendar.*
- How to work with—or around—a high Stimulation and Excitement Quota.

Every human being needs stimulation to survive. That's a proven psychological fact. Without attention, recognition, and contact, we will wither on the vine like a flower denied access to light and water. In addition, many of us need a more intense form of stimulation—we need excitement!

The Excitement of the Last-Minute Rush

I am acquainted with a father of five who regularly packs his family into their minivan for a drive to dinner or some event. Every so often he delays stopping for gas until the tank is dangerously close to empty. Then he careens down the road driving in a zigzag pattern "to get the edges of the gas into the tank." The kids crane their necks to spot an open service station. His wife shudders. The air crackles with excitement. The anxiety level is high. The children cheer as they finally pull into a station. You would think this man would get enough excitement in his job as chairman of a corporation with over 50 operations across the country, but his Stimulation and Excitement Quota (S&EQ) is off the chart.

Different Stimulation and Excitement Quotas

We all have our own individual S&EQ. How we fill it affects our time. We get what we need in different ways. An elderly widow adds a dash of excitement to her quiet life with a last-minute flurry of arrangements for her monthly bridge party. A Broadway star dashes in just before curtain time and throws dozens of people into an uproar every night as they breathlessly help her get ready for the performance. One requires relatively little stimulation and excitement, the other a great deal.

We all fill our quota, whether we do it knowingly or unknowingly, positively or negatively. However, negative stimulation and excitement can produce harmful stress. Negative excitement doesn't come cheap. It can take a heavy toll emotionally and physically—on ourselves and others.

Let's probe into the hidden psychological reasons why some of us seek negative stimulation and excitement, and explore ways we can change that by filling our quotas positively. I will show you, as I have shown many others in my seminars, how to maintain the level of stimulation and excitement you need in productive rather than destructive ways.

Filling a Temporary Void

Sometimes, people seek negative stimulation because of a temporary lack in positive stimulation. That's what led Carole into a situation that could have hurt her career.

Carole's former boss took pride in pointing out that she was one of the few women at her level of management in a major utilities company. He encouraged her and gave her work high visibility. Carole thrived until a new manager took over.

Her new manager believed in a "leave them alone" leadership style. He rarely talked with Carole about her work. He was sparing in praise. After four months of this treatment, Carole found herself missing deadlines. For the first time in her life, she was leaving work until the last minute. She hated the stress, but didn't know why she was acting this way. Her boss reprimanded her. She scolded herself. Things just got worse. She fell farther behind. Then one evening at home, when Carole was sitting at her dining table doing some planning, she saw the connection. She realized the root of her problem. She realized she was at least getting attention.

Now Carole makes sure she gets the positive attention she needs to do a good job. She's developed a support group among her peers and people in other departments. They are happy when she calls to tell them about a new accomplishment. She keeps her S&EQ on "full" from these sources. She respects her manager's style, but she also understands her own needs.

Stimulation is a basic need, one we all share. It doesn't show lack of maturity to seek it. Healthy human beings recognize the need. They learn how to take care of it productively.

Getting Everybody into the Act

Some of us can get our stimulation on our own. We can give ourselves a pat on the back, add zest to the day by taking a walk in the woods, or derive excitement from planning a birthday surprise for someone we love. For those with a higher excitement level, singular stimulation isn't enough. Many need a barrage of crises to generate the intense excitement they like.

A politician has a major address scheduled months in advance. His staff does all the backup work, but they can never get him to sit down and hammer out the final speech. Somehow, something always gets in the way. The day before the event, he involves all of them in a 24-hour speech-writing marathon. The crisis generates the excitement he needs to be "up" for his appearance. He makes a brilliant presentation. But his staff is drained, exhausted, and left to pick up the pieces.

Negative excitement can extract a high toll from others. Eventually, the support troops may decide it's not worth it.

Deeper Roots of Defiance

People who habitually seek negative stimulation are often reacting to drives that stem from childhood patterns of defiance. Defiance is a habitual reaction against perceived authority. There are many degrees of defiance. I have seen many successful salespeople, trial attorneys, and entrepreneurs who are defiant.

These patterns evolve from three basic decisions early in life: "I'll show 'em," "You can't make me," and "I'll do it my way." Whether in response to spoken or nonverbal communication, they are the child's way of coping with messages that seem to say, "You'll never make it," "You must do it my way," or "You can't do it."

A little girl reacts to her father's suggestion that she wear an angel costume to the kindergarten costume party by insisting she wants to be a witch instead. She wants to do it her way. A boy doesn't rebel openly when his mother calls, "Come in for dinner now." He just responds, "In a minute," and drags that minute out as long as he can. He's showing her that she can't make him. A child whose older brother tells him he's too clumsy to join the baseball team defiantly practices batting at odd hours until he's good enough to make the team.

An early decision to "show 'em" is often the key to survival for a young child. He or she resolves to make it in spite of all obstacles. Later in life, some may continue to react this way. Even when it's not appropriate or helpful, they make every project a struggle. They constantly feel they have to prove something.

The Struggle Against Structure—Lists, Calendars, and Deadlines

People who exhibit defiant behavior continually struggle against structure in their lives. They view lists, calendars, and deadlines as objects to defy. They lose lists constantly and can't take the time to keep a calendar. When they have a deadline, they rarely meet it. Even if they set the deadline themselves, they don't see it as something to be met. Unconsciously, they perceive it as one more opportunity to "show 'em," to succeed "in spite of." They aren't aware of it, but they are so used to overcoming obstacles that they create them even when they don't exist.

People who habitually react with defiance will move mountains to overcome an "insurmountable" obstacle. But they'll yawn when faced with an important task that seems too easy. They're bored. Even if the result is desirable, they aren't interested. Grabbing for the challenge is what triggers their enthusiasm.

There's no doubt that an "I'll show 'em" reaction offers some rewards. The determination to overcome obstacles can contribute to success in a competitive society like ours. Defiant people refuse to accept temporary defeat. They struggle eternally against the odds, real or artificially produced. They develop a kind of energy and stamina that adds an edge in many situations.

Yet despite the rewards it can offer, defiant behavior has a darker side. It usually involves "cutting off your nose to spite your face." This darker side can set up rigid behavior patterns. When every aspect of life is seen as a contest, many avenues of growth and feeling are cut off. Personal fulfillment is blocked. This type of behavior is enormously wasteful in terms of human potential. It can rob you of quality time in some of the most important areas of your life.

If the roots of defiant behavior are deep, overnight change is unlikely. I have found prayer and good counseling that helps heal defiance well worth the time and money.

If you have a defiance problem, you can begin to work on it by substituting positive behavior that will fill your Stimulation and Excitement Quota more creatively. It's a relief to know you don't always have to struggle or suffer to pay for good times and good feelings. It's good to know you don't ever have to do anything to hurt yourself.

Fill Your S&EQ Creatively

When you understand why you seek negative stimulation and excitement, it is easier to create ways to fill your quota positively. The following case illustrates how one man did it.

Although Len was an officer in a Fortune 500 company, he confessed to having more than 30 years of practice in defiant behavior. The long habits of constant struggle and last-minute rushes kept his S&EQ filled. The toll was high, however, and he wanted to find a better way. He realized he needed a considerable amount of excitement, so he decided to discover positive ways to get it.

One Sunday afternoon Len sat down with a pot of coffee and a lined yellow pad. An hour later he'd created a blueprint for satisfying his needs more creatively. Here's what his list contained:

1. Put at least one exciting activity on the calendar every day.

2. Use outside resources to help expand ideas for solving business problems: investment bankers, other financial officers, consultants, data research services, books, and articles.

3. Do some work at different levels and in different areas to provide variety: Spend some time in conceptual planning, some in people managing, some in a detailed project, and some on manual work (like building shelves for the garage).

4. Vary outside activities to include involvement with people in all walks of life: Volunteer for the community fund drive, attend a city council meeting, join a church group, or sign up as a Boy Scout troop leader.

5. Schedule time regularly with the children, individually and all together: Take Erik to a football game, Ashley to a Saturday matineę, Ellen to field hockey, and all of them for a picnic at the beach.

6. Have an active and varied social life: spend some time with one person, some in groups; set aside time for both structured and unstructured activities.

7. Book interesting things ahead: Subscribe to the symphony series, get football season tickets, and make reservations for a singer who's coming to town.

This list was only the beginning for Len, but it put him on the right track. He realized that only by substituting positive stimulation and excitement could he wean himself away from those old negative behavior patterns he wanted to change. Your Stimulation and Excitement Quota may be lower than Len's—or higher. Whatever the level, you can use a similar approach to fill it creatively and positively.

You Have a Choice

What can you do if you have an important person in your life with time problems rooted in defiance? It helps to understand that their actions aren't deliberate, but you don't have to suffer because of their unintentional behavior.

Take a good look at the benefits you get from the relationship and consider what it costs you. Think about the costs and benefits involved for the other person. Understand the dynamics of his or her unproductive behavior, and don't reward and reinforce it. You can relate to that person constructively and still take care of yourself.

David has been happily married for 17 years to Margaret, a woman notorious for being late. He told me how he learned to live with her time habits:

> Margaret is an admirable woman in many ways. I delight in her company. I realized years ago, however, that I'd have to find a way to work around her time problems. I now have a backup plan, and I don't let her lateness frustrate me.
>
> When Margaret and I set a specific time to meet, I know she'll be at least 20 minutes late. She always has an explanation—usually just one more thing to do before leaving. I used to wait on street corners. I'd stand there breathing in traffic fumes and building up anger while waiting for her to arrive. I'd be so irritated, I wouldn't

enjoy the first hour of our time together. Over the years, I learned this never helped.

Now I pick a place where I won't mind waiting. Sometimes I choose an interesting hotel lobby where I can work or watch people going by. Other times, I find a favorite restaurant. I can contemplate the menu and setting until Margaret shows up.

If you're part of a similar situation, be realistic. Provide yourself with a backup plan. Figure out ways to make that waiting time enjoyable. Pray for healing of this habit. Focus on what is important to you in the relationship, and move the other person's time problems to the periphery. They may not change their old habits, but you can find a way to do what is best for your time. The choice is yours.

Keep a Clear Perspective

Every human being needs stimulation and excitement to survive. It is a sign of maturity to recognize this need and take care of it.

- We all have different Stimulation and Excitement Quotas. Recognize what your S&EQ is and discover how you are currently filling it. Face up to mixed feelings in yourself and others.

- Understand the plus side and minus side of defiant behavior in yourself and those around you.

- Learn to fill your Stimulation and Excitement Quota in positive ways to free more time for enjoying what counts most to you. You can prevent this time loss and also the drain of time from another threat in the next chapter.

Chapter 7

How Slippery Guilt Drains Time

*If we confess our sins, he is faithful and just to forgive us our sins,
and to cleanse us from all unrighteousness.*

1 John 1:9 KJV

What's Ahead

- Two kinds of time-wasting guilt.
- How to spring the guilt trap.
- What happens when you bring guilt to God.

Guilt is implicated in more wasted time and poor time arrangement than any other single emotion. That is why it's vital to understand the two types of guilt—real guilt and slippery guilt—and the relationship between guilt and time.

Don't Let Cultural Guilt Cloud Your Thinking

The person voicing the following description of guilt speaks for many of us:

> When I finally sit down to concentrate on something important, I'm plagued with guilty feelings about a dozen other things—the mess around me, the letters I

haven't written, the calls I must make, the people I should see, the chores I haven't done. So I get up and attend to something I feel guilty about. Then I'm out of the mood to concentrate. So I never have enough time to do what's really important.

A Messy Desk Is the Sign of a Messy Desk

Even though many people feel guilty about a messy desk, numerous cases reveal that there is no direct correlation between neatness and productivity. Some very productive people have papers stacked all over their desks; others have absolutely none. The real issue is accomplishing the work that's most important to you. However, if you are a Category Two who needs to concentrate to be orderly, you may need to have your desk cleaner than your Category One colleagues. Cultural guilt and a messy desk are so common, there is probably a market for a bumper sticker that reads: "A messy desk is a sign of a messy desk." It could help someone who has clutter but can still find things skip the guilt.

When we feel guilty, we don't do our best thinking. We often end up in a flurry of activity on matters that are not of central importance. We may even add the suffocating grip of inaction. Despite a massive attack of painful guilt, we don't do anything. We put off doing what is really important—sometimes until it is too late.

Before we go further, here is my definition of guilt: A feeling of deviation from a relevant standard. I use the word "relevant" because we feel guilty only when we have not fulfilled a standard for which we believe we are responsible.

When we succumb to guilt feelings, we set up a barrier to effective time use. You can overcome this barrier more easily when you understand the two kinds of guilt, and why some guilt feelings are often inappropriate.

Two Kinds of Guilt

Guilt *can* be real and appropriate. If someone commits murder, batters a child, or steals another's life savings, these are true reasons to feel guilty. Whatever the subject of the guilt, the response is clear. Confess your transgression to God, ask for His forgiveness, and accept His forgiveness.

God gives us a great privilege in confession. When I thought confession wasn't that important, Elizabeth challenged me to sit down some Sunday afternoon and read the book of Psalms and see what it says about confession. It says a lot. The book of Proverbs spotlights confession also.

> You will never succeed in life if you try to hide your sins. Confess them and give them up; then God will show mercy to you (Proverbs 28:13 TEV).

If you are like many people who feel drained by guilt, memorize the following Bible quote to prompt you to confess, ask for forgiveness, and accept God's forgiveness.

> If we confess our sins, he is faithful and just to forgive us our sins, and to cleanse us from all unrighteousness (1 John 1:9 KJV).

At this point, someone usually raises a hand and objects: "What about those people who do something wrong, confess it, and then go back and do it again and again?"

Of course, the response here is: Don't you be one of those people. God is asking you to be responsible for yourself and not your neighbor down the street. So commit yourself to confess, ask for forgiveness, accept it, and also let your repentance show in your actions as Paul teaches.

> [I] kept declaring both to those of Damascus first, and also at Jerusalem and then throughout all the region of Judea, and even to the Gentiles, that they should repent and turn to God, performing deeds appropriate to repentance (Acts 26:20 NASB).

What if you have done all this and you are like many people who still feel guilty? At this point, we must stand on the truth that God has given to us who believe and trust Him as Savior and Lord.

> Therefore there is now no condemnation for those who
> are in Christ Jesus (Romans 8:1 NASB).

This is the perfect moment to turn a time of slippery cultural guilt into a time of praise to God. "You are a God of forgiveness. You are a generous God. You are a God of great love." We can continue with thanksgiving: "Thank You for Your forgiveness. Thank You for Your promises in the Bible. Thank You for Your love for me." Then put your mental energies into memorizing quotes from the Bible and hiding God's Word in your heart.

Now we are on to the biggest time drain—slippery, phony guilt that is not from God but rather from our culture.

How to Spot Slippery Guilt

This remaining guilt robs people of their time and energy. It isn't real guilt. It's phony because it's inappropriate. It's slippery. Dolores finally cleans the closet she has been feeling guilty about. Moments after she shuts the door on the closet, she starts to feel guilty about the thank-you notes she has not written. As soon as she writes the notes, she feels guilty about not returning a dinner invitation. This type of slippery guilt wastes time and drains energy.

Symptoms of inappropriate guilt spring from many different causes. Some people feel guilty if they don't do everything perfectly or don't keep busy every moment. Others feel guilty about enjoying themselves or about feeling good when someone else is unhappy. Some people may even feel guilty about feeling guilty.

Most of the time-wasting guilt feelings we allow to intrude on our time are related to the less important situations or chores—a messy back closet, an overflowing garage, a dinner invitation, or the need to catch up on current events.

Examine your own guilt feelings carefully. You may find they are generated by a failure to meet an outdated standard. At one time that standard may have been meaningful, but it is now inappropriate.

The Treadmill of Busyness—
An Outdated Standard

After a recent speech I made to a professional association, an old acquaintance came up and asked, "Are you busy these days?" In the preceding months, I'd managed to achieve a rewarding balance between work and recreation. It was with a real sense of accomplishment that I replied, "No, I'm not busy all the time." Much to my chagrin, my acquaintance looked embarrassed. He backed away, muttering, "I'm sure things will get better—you'll be busy again soon." Before I could explain, he beat a hasty retreat.

His remark reflected the old cultural standard that glorifies busyness. He didn't consider whether my energies were well directed or productive, nor what I was accomplishing with my time.

Comments like this can also have deeper meanings. For example, consider the statement, "I'm so busy I never have a minute to myself." How often have you heard variations on that theme? Such comments may really mean, "I'm busy, therefore I'm needed. I'm worthwhile." Busyness becomes the standard people use to measure their worth as human beings. They believe it's the only way to justify their existence. Jane was busy at her job as a nurse, as a basketball mom, and as a wife. Sometimes when she tries to slow down, she remembers her mother's voice telling her when she was a small child, "I almost died when you were born." Then Jane redoubles her busy efforts to make up for what she feels she did to her mother. Jane knows intellectually that a little baby does not "almost kill" her mother, but she still feels guilty. So after years of struggle, she now reminds herself daily that her feelings are important, but the fact of God's love and care is more important.

Personal worth does not depend upon what you do. You have value as a human being regardless of your activities. The prestige or economic value of your work has no bearing on your worth or your right to human dignity. If these two issues are confused, it's common to fall into the trap of feeling guilty about what you do or don't do with your time. The real issue is to understand that you deserve to be here and that you matter to God.

The Perfection Syndrome

Preoccupation with hard work and busyness isn't the only standard that can produce inappropriate guilt. Many of us further burden ourselves by the perfection syndrome. People in this snare feel they must do everything perfectly. They strive to maintain the cleanest house in town and the neatest desk in their department. Their lives are so completely organized that every task must be finished, and finished perfectly.

The media bombards us with images that contribute to these inappropriate standards of perfection. Television and magazine ads show us floors that always gleam, people who never slouch or get fat, children whose clothes are always clean and wrinkle free.

If you make such standards a part of your life, you are setting yourself up to carry a heavy load of guilt. You lose the ability to make thoughtful judgments about your work. You are likely to waste enormous amounts of time on tasks that don't really matter.

I Should Have Done Better

This concept is an offshoot of the perfection syndrome. The problem is that most people who use this phrase don't even define what "better" means. They fall short of the standard without ever knowing what the standard is.

I once worked with a dedicated senior executive who continually plagued himself with feelings of guilt about not "doing better." No matter how much he accomplished, he never felt it was enough. He'd become a chronic workaholic. His family hardly knew what he looked like. He wanted to change, but he didn't know how to free himself from guilt.

Then one day after one of his staff members was leaving his office, he sat at his conference table, looked at the door, and thought about the discussion he had just finished. As he started to feel as though he should have done more, he realized that he was denying himself the courtesy he had extended to the man who just left. Defining what the standard is. Knowing where the dangling carrot is. Yet, he had never clearly defined exactly what "better" meant in his own situation.

He sat down and analyzed his job responsibilities. He defined exactly what and how much he was responsible for. He set specific standards for measuring his performance so he would know if and when he missed the mark.

He didn't change overnight. He's been following his new regime for several months now, but he still feels an occasional twinge of guilt when he walks out of his office at 5:30 P.M. and sees members of his staff still working on their projects. But he keeps right on walking. He reminds himself, "I concentrate on doing what is most important; I don't let guilt feelings run my life." He can deal with the guilt feelings now; it gets easier every day. And he knows he's not wasting his time on inappropriate guilt.

Portable Guilt

Guilt arising from standards that are unrealistic, irrelevant, and ill-defined is a slippery enemy. If you clean up the messy drawer you feel guilty about, you might find you now feel guilty about that pile of magazines you haven't read yet. One thing leads to another. Don't believe you can ever satisfy free-floating, unrealistic guilt by "doing better," "doing more," or "doing enough." There will always be something else to feel guilty about.

Springing the Guilt Trap

Even if you feel guilty, go ahead and do what you know is most important. Continuing, constructive action toward what really counts remedies inappropriate guilt. Ask yourself this question when you are feeling guilty: "Have I confessed this to God, asked for His forgiveness, accepted His forgiveness, and showed my repentance in my actions?"

If you have done this, then ask the next questions.

1. Specifically, what am I feeling guilty about?

2. Is this something that is really an essential or central concern to me or to someone else?

3. Today, how can I best do what really counts?

The answers to these questions will help you grasp the keys to successful time investment: identifying the central concerns in your life, understanding the motivation involved, and doing what really counts every day. These are the major themes of this book, and they will be developed in detail in later chapters. The techniques you will learn will help you do the right things at the right times without letting guilt feelings run your life. God created joy. You deserve to feel joy. You can have fun.

Doing What Really Counts

If you wait until you have done all the little things you feel guilty about, you may never get to the heart of what really counts. A painful situation I wish had not been true brought this lesson home to me.

"This afternoon they told Margaret she has only one more week to live." The words I was hearing over the telephone stunned me. David was telling me that Margaret, his wife and my special friend, was dying. The doctors had finally diagnosed the source of her sudden streak of splitting headaches as "increased intracranial pressure secondary to a brain tumor."

It sounded unreal; I couldn't believe it. Margaret was only 42. I couldn't believe that she might die so suddenly, in such a cruelly unexpected way.

I'd seen her just four weeks earlier. She had been as blithe and full of vitality as ever. She and her husband had an exceptionally happy marriage, two wonderful sons, rewarding careers—everything to live for.

A poignant memory of Margaret illustrates how her concentration on what was most important to her brought beauty to others.

One day when I was visiting her, she pointed to a framed rubbing on their living room wall and told me what she and her husband did with their young sons. They made rubbings of late nineteenth-century manhole covers together. Every Saturday they would board the subway armed with rice paper, tape, brushes, and charcoal. They'd head for one of the older neighborhoods in the city where there were some unusual and historic manhole covers. When they discovered one they liked, they'd get right down to work. One of the boys would brush away the dirt, the other would tape down the rice paper. Inevitably, their activity would attract a crowd of children, curious to know what two adults and two boys were doing crouched over a manhole.

Margaret smiled as she related how fascinated the neighborhood children would become. She knew it helped them see their neighborhood in a different way. She loved the idea that as a result of her family's activity, these children became more alive to the beauty of ordinary, everyday things in the world around them, and when her children looked at the rubbing on their living room wall, they would be reminded of their times together.

Long after the call ended, I sat thinking about Margaret. I remembered visiting her at home another day. Her desk in the corner of the family study was overflowing with papers. She laughed as she gestured toward it and said, "I guess I should feel guilty about how messy it looks, but there are so many things more important to me than having a clean desk."

Two weeks after the first call from her husband, I ran upstairs to my room in the hotel where I was speaking. As I sat on the bed and called the hospital, David handed her the telephone. Even though painkilling drugs slowed her familiar voice to halting phrases, her words rang with unquenchable spirit and profound wisdom.

Margaret did not get a miracle reprieve. But in that call two days before her death, she told me, "For some reason, during these last six months, I've been thinking more about how I spend my time. I'd always thought of myself as primarily career-oriented, but I now realize that my family is most important to me. I've been concentrating on spending more time with them."

As I sat on the hotel bed, gripping the phone, struggling to control my tears, Margaret went on to say something that has made a difference in my life each day since.

"It's so much easier to face what I am facing now because I've spent my time on what really counts."

As I sat by the phone, reliving my memories of my friend, I thought over what she had said to me about doing what counts. I realized that if I were in a similar situation, I couldn't make that statement. I was not spending my time on the things that really mattered. I was allowing too much of it to slip away on small things I felt guilty about.

The lesson is clear. Skip the phony guilt. Go directly to what counts. Do the right things at the right times.

Skip the Slippery Guilt. Do What Really Counts

It's important to clearly identify the source of any guilt feelings. When you have real guilt, confess it to God and ask for His forgiveness. When you have an invitation to feel phony cultural guilt, don't accept it. You are in charge of your feelings.

Every day continue to do what counts. Do it first, even if it means putting off secondary matters, doing them less perfectly, getting someone else to do them, or not doing them at all.

God has given you this day. Accept it. Use it. Enjoy it. Thank God for it...even when you discover how long ago some of your time patterns started.

Chapter 8

Mom, Dad, and Your Time Today

*Remember the LORD in everything you do,
and he will show you the right way.*
Proverbs 3:6 TEV

What's Ahead

- How old messages can impact your time today.
- The big-time benefits of becoming aware of early messages.

As a child, you received many messages about time from your parents. They may have been positive or negative, clear or mixed, spoken or nonverbal. These messages may even vary for different children in the same family. The ideas we absorb are always highly individual, but what they have in common is impact.

Although many people are unaware that early childhood experiences influence their time today, they repeat day after day patterns learned long ago. This chapter will help you discover what early messages you learned, how they influence your time as an adult, and how to change them if you want to.

Sorting Out the Messages

Sometimes, the productive messages parents communicate are verbal. Betty, a financial executive in a large corporation, told me that one of her mother's favorite sayings contributed to her success. She grew up hearing the gentle but firm reminder, "duty first." As a child, she learned to finish her work before she went out to play. Today that old message, "duty first," helps her organize her priorities. She's earned a well-deserved reputation for consistently getting the right things done on time.

Another successful woman in the same company never actually heard anyone say, "duty first," but she got the message anyway. Her mother was a legal secretary who worked five days a week and had an hour's daily commute. Grocery shopping was done on Saturdays, and her mother insisted that household chores and getting the house ready for Sunday came before outings or excursions. The children learned that if they wanted to speed up departure time for a trip to the amusement park or the beach, they had to help with the housecleaning first.

Jim, a real estate broker, consulted me about a problem that had been plaguing him all his life. He wasted enormous amounts of time struggling to get himself going on the job each day. When he recalled how his parents used time, he got in touch with the beginnings of his problem. His father put off things from Sunday to Saturday. When minor repairs around the house needed attention, his father took months to get around to them. The summer window screens would still be up in November. The storm windows weren't taken down until July. The Christmas tree was still standing in February. As a child, Jim got the message, "You can always do it tomorrow." Unconsciously, he was complicating his time by following that unproductive message as an adult.

Same Message—Different Route

Many people receive the same messages in different ways. One child may hear, "Keep busy! Idle hands are the devil's workshop!" and develop a preoccupation with busyness in later life. This message might produce fear or distrust of unstructured leisure. It may even interfere with wholehearted enjoyment of good times.

Another child may never have heard that old motto, but he will pick up the same message. Perhaps he observed his parents in a never-ending stream of busy activities: his mother knitting wherever she went; his father invariably bringing home a briefcase stuffed with work. As an adult, this child may develop similar habits. He may believe that he, too, must always keep busy. He doesn't know that you can be childlike at times and have fun frequently.

Mixed Messages

Although some messages are clear, others can be mixed. Parents may say one thing, but do another, like that old proverb "Do as I say, not as I do." The child is not always able to make the distinction.

Philip is an executive in an advertising firm. His world is filled with deadlines, but for years he constantly struggled with them. When Philip learned to understand childhood messages, he discovered the root of his problem. He explained that both his parents were forever harping on the importance of being on time. Their actions, however, communicated another message.

If the family was setting out for an appointment or an excursion, the same thing always happened. The parents would nag the children to hurry up, get ready, and get in the car. Philip and his two brothers would pile into the car, all set to go. Invariably, they'd have to wait for their parents. Dad would take time to wind up the garden hose. Mom would make one last tour through the house, checking that all the doors were locked. They were rarely on time anywhere. What they did, rather than what they said, formed the message for Philip.

Deliberate or Not, It Still Makes a Difference

As you learned in the previous chapter, we don't deliberately seek negative stimulation and excitement, but sometimes such behavior stems from watching our parents seek negative stimulation. Remember the father of five lurching his vehicle back and forth in a zigzag pattern to get the last of the gas into the engine? As they rounded every curve in the road, nervously scouting the horizon for a service station, his children were receiving a strong message. Their father was showing them a negative way to get stimulation and excitement.

Some children resort to negative stimulation because positive sources aren't readily available. A child who receives little or no attention or praise from his parents for constructive behavior soon discovers the rewards of negative behavior. A series of "accidents" may occur. A fishbowl is knocked over. Scissors are dropped down the toilet. A peanut butter and jelly sandwich is found mashed into the rug. The child gets attention and life is suddenly more exciting. The seeds of negative stimulation have been sown.

Some learn to give negative stimulation to themselves as an adult. When Dana was growing up, her mother constantly told her how she should improve. "Why are you always late? You should know better. How could you?" Her mother added little love and acceptance to balance the instruction. As an adult, Dana played both parts. She would tell herself, "Why are you always late? You should know better," and deliver her internal scoldings and negative stimulation before feeling familiar whipped-puppy feelings.

One day when she was late to a morning meeting, her car's gas gauge was on empty and her hair was undone. She recognized she was giving herself a lecture with her mother's exact tone and wording. As she was driving back home that night, she continued listening to her internal messages and realized what she was doing. The next morning in her car, she decided on a two-step plan. First she stopped beating herself up—even if she was late—so there was no "need" to be late to earn the familiar scolding. Then she started finding things she had done well and congratulated herself for those areas. She was determined, and she kept withholding the negative and adding the congratulations while doing things to arrive early. This way, she gradually weaned herself from the unhealthy old habit of being late to gain some stimulation.

What Messages Did You Learn?

Here are some of the most common areas of psychological programming relating to time. What messages did you pick up about these subjects when you were a child?

- Being on time

- Being late

- Not finishing on time

- Clocks

- Duty first

- Negative attention

- Promptness

- Being early

- Knowing when to leave

- Arriving ahead of time

- Being the first one there

- Being the last to leave

- Being the first to leave

- Dawdling

Are there any other messages about time that come to mind? What impact do they have on your time use today?

Take a few minutes to consider what you learned about time while you were growing up. Discover which messages are still helpful and identify those that no longer serve you well.

You can change if you desire. For example, Jim, who watched his father procrastinate from Sunday to Saturday, takes great delight in telling himself, "I do it now" as he takes down the Christmas tree on New Year's Day. Nicole heard her father roar to the family on Sunday mornings, "We're all going to be late!"

Now she tells herself in the evening, "It's fun to be ready the night before," as she hangs her outfit on the closet door and makes sure she is prepared for her class.

Candy, whose parents arrived at dinners and meetings early and parked around the corner until the exact time, likes her childhood example and enjoys parking around the corner today.

Reinforce the Best

- Identify the messages you learned about time while you were growing up.

- Remember that although childhood is a strong influence, you need not let it dictate adult behavior. You can change your behavior today if you choose to do so.

- Most habits—productive or nonproductive—stem from repetition and reinforcement. That's why they can be changed through repetition and reinforcement.

Chapter 9

The Few Techniques That Free You from Compulsive Time

I will give thanks to You, for I am fearfully and wonderfully made.
Psalm 139:14 NASB

What's Ahead

- Why some habits are hard to change.
- Five time styles and the plus and minus of each.
- How to find the few time tools that will give you the best results.
- The wonderful potential of Choice Time.

Have you ever wondered why one person will hear about a new time tool and immediately put it into action, while an equally bright person in a similar situation does not? The second person may think the tool is a good idea—may even start to use it a few times. However, he or she lets it drop, never reaping the benefits. Why? The answer usually lies in the difference between Choice Time and Compulsive Time.

Dealing from Blind Spots

People who don't put relevant time techniques to work for themselves are often operating from a blind spot. They have let themselves fall into the habit of inefficient Compulsive Time use.

For example, two specialists in the same company were exposed to a classic time technique—handle papers only once. Both men said it would help reduce their workload, but each had a different response.

One of the men put it to work immediately and revolutionized his paperwork. "For the first time in my career, my desk looks civilized. The idea makes such common sense, I don't know why I didn't think of it myself."

However, the other specialist still wrestled with a flood of paperwork. "I thought that handling papers once was a good idea when I first heard it. But here I am—still drowning in paper in a paperless world. I go through my incoming box a dozen times, pick something up, and look at it. Then I wonder if I have enough information, so I put it down again. I know I should handle each document only once, but it's not that easy. And it's the same problem with my email in-basket."

This dynamic crops up hundreds of times in time seminars. It explains why so many intelligent people fail to put time techniques to work for themselves. What's "just common sense" to one person remains out of reach for someone else.

Compulsive Time use is part of the human condition. It merely means that many of us feel compelled to function in a habitual way even when it is not helpful. For example, a person may feel compelled to hurry all the time, even when he is eating his plate of barbecue at a picnic. At these times, how we act overshadows the purpose of our actions.

Consider yourself. What are some of the time tools you know but rarely use? Examine your own time patterns in this light, and you will discover some important and revealing patterns. You're on track to understanding your areas of Compulsive Time use.

Choosing the Best Techniques

Here's the delightful reality. You don't need to use all the time techniques in this book. You only need to concentrate on the few that will help you deal with your blind spots—your Compulsive

Time uses. The other techniques will seem natural to you. You'll put them to work almost without thought.

"What's Wrong with Compulsive Time?"

Compulsive Time use is not necessarily negative, it's just less than the best. It's not the most effective or efficient. You don't do your clearest thinking when you are operating from compulsion. You block yourself from getting the optimum return on your time investment. You can accomplish what you want through Compulsive Time use, but you pay a higher price.

You achieve better results when you learn to transfer your energies to Choice Time. What's more, you will achieve those greater results faster, more easily, and with increased satisfaction.

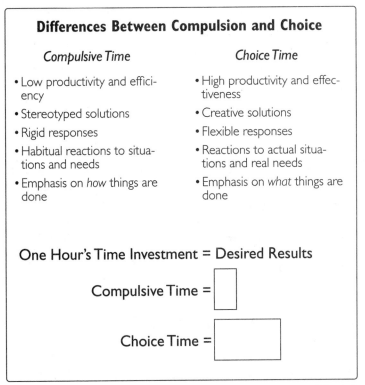

Differences Between Compulsion and Choice

Compulsive Time	*Choice Time*
• Low productivity and efficiency	• High productivity and effectiveness
• Stereotyped solutions	• Creative solutions
• Rigid responses	• Flexible responses
• Habitual reactions to situations and needs	• Reactions to actual situations and real needs
• Emphasis on *how* things are done	• Emphasis on *what* things are done

One Hour's Time Investment = Desired Results

Compulsive Time = ☐

Choice Time = ☐

Fig. 9.1

Diagnosing your own Compulsive Time use is the first step toward gaining more Choice Time. It frees you to choose techniques that will reduce your Compulsive Time use.

Five Types of Compulsive Time

The psychological theory of five major types of compulsive behavior was developed for therapeutic application by Taibi Kahler, a brilliant psychologist from Little Rock, Arkansas. He chose the following highly descriptive titles for each type: Hurry Up, Be Perfect, Please, Try Hard, and Be Strong.[1]

When I first encountered Dr. Kahler's theory, it seemed too simplistic, although I knew that he had achieved remarkable results. I objected to the idea that there were "only" five roles. Surely my experience would reveal several others.

In the years that followed, I became convinced that Dr. Kahler was correct. His theory clearly illustrates how extensive psychological material can be condensed into nontechnical language. Furthermore, I discovered that his theory applied to time as well.

Some of the five types will seem more familiar to you than others. Although we engage in all of them some of the time, most of us specialize in two roles. Spot the two that fit your use of time most closely.

Remember, you don't have to use hundreds of time tools, only those that relate to your most frequent Compulsive Time uses. Techniques that relate to Choice Time will seem just like common sense. You may be using them already without realizing it.

After each description, I have listed some of the techniques that are most helpful in reducing that type of compulsive behavior. Use these brief lists as a handy guide for selecting the techniques you want to learn.

Hurry Up

People playing a Hurry Up role rush whether it's necessary or not. They rush to work. They rush to meet deadlines. They rush to a picnic. If they have two days to accomplish something, they'll find a way to delay starting until just before the deadline.

They collect a large amount of excitement from rushing. It isn't always the best way to get the stimulation they need, and it isn't usually a necessary or efficient investment of time.

A successful salesman who plays a Hurry Up role built his original ten small accounts into a total of 30. Now 15 of them generate 90 percent of his income. However, he runs himself ragged servicing all 30 accounts. He doesn't stop to realize that this isn't the best way to invest his time and energy. He could turn over the 15 smaller accounts to a less experienced person on the sales staff, and he'd have the time to develop even larger accounts. But he still hangs on to the 30.

Some Techniques to Reduce the Hurry Up Role:

- Do Central Concerns and Essential Priorities first.

- Carve out time each day for perspective and planning.

- First clarify what you want to accomplish before deciding how to do it.

- Study your personal calendar whenever you have a spare moment of Time In.

- Fill your personal Stimulation and Excitement Quota positively. Plan your time with this desire in mind.

- Set deadlines for steps rather than only one final deadline.

Be Perfect

People who play a Be Perfect role waste valuable time on trivial or marginal matters because they feel they must perform every task perfectly. A competent graduate student redoes all her notes on the computer. She dusts her desk twice a day. She stands in front of her closet for minutes deciding what to wear to class. She works beyond the point of diminishing return on everything. She told me that she vividly recalled her father's response whenever she brought home a school paper marked "96 percent" or even "98 percent." Invariably, he'd smile, shake a finger at her, and say, "Why not 100 percent?"

Be Perfects also have difficulty admitting a mistake, and they waste time defending it or trying to cover it up.

Their ability to make decisions suffers as well. Every decision must be perfect, even on an inconsequential matter. One group of Be Perfects worked on a committee to prepare a project report. They spent 60 minutes one day deciding whether to label the report's supplemental material "Attachment" or "Tab." They were intelligent, competent, analytical people, but they were playing the Be Perfect role.

In their personal lives, people assuming a Be Perfect role seek out perfect relationships. They spend considerable time searching for the ideal man or the ideal woman. At the first sign of clay feet on their latest idol, they leave, compelled to find someone else. Since ideal men and women are rare, their search is never ending.

Stacks of newspapers and magazines often surround the perfectionist. If you feel that you have to read everything, it's easy to generate a backlog of reading.

Accountants and lawyers often play Be Perfect roles. If you just want a rough financial estimate, a Be Perfect accountant will provide a detailed report that took five hours to prepare. You will receive much more information than you need to reach your decision. If you ask a Be Perfect lawyer for some general business advice, you will wind up with an exhaustive, heavily annotated summary of the Uniform Commercial Code.

People playing Be Perfect roles often postpone completion of a project because of their compulsion to do everything perfectly. Scientists and engineers may work on a project for six months and compile enough data to produce 90 percent of their findings. But they'll feel compelled to spend 12 more months perfecting that last ten percent. Others may postpone a project entirely because they know they can't do it perfectly.

Some Techniques to Reduce the Be Perfect Role

• Avoid perfectionism on things that are secondary or marginal.

- Handle papers only once, or at least take some action each time you pick them up.

- Use headlines in books and magazines as signposts for material to read in detail.

- If you waste time searching for something, find a substitute whenever possible.

- Estimate how much time projects are really worth to you and stick to your estimate.

- Every day, deliberately do at least something imperfectly.

Please

Do you frequently say yes when you want to say no? You're probably playing a Please role. Please types often have the best intentions in the world. They don't want to hurt someone's feelings. They hate to give bad news. They don't want people to dislike them. Therefore, Please types frequently overcommit themselves. They say yes to so many people that they aren't able to deliver all they promise. They wind up disappointing others and hurting themselves.

Gene was working on a government grant, and his project director fell into the Please role. This Please person knew for months that the grant would not be renewed, but he avoided telling his staff. He didn't want them to worry and hated giving bad news. As a result, no one on the staff was prepared for the funding cutoff date. None had taken time to update their résumés or start finding another job.

When I first came to work in San Francisco, I let myself fall into the Please trap. I was right out of college and suddenly conscious of my student appearance. I wanted a more professional image for my job, and buying a coat for the cool San Francisco summer was my first step. After spending a long time trying on coats with a saleswoman, I let myself get talked into buying a mustard brown coat with a high collar. At the time, my look included tortoiseshell glasses, no makeup, and mousy brown hair. With that coat I looked like a big hot dog. But I didn't want to hurt the saleswoman's feelings, so to please her I bought it. Today, whenever I find myself falling into Please behavior, one mental flash of that mustard coat clears my thinking.

Some Techniques to Reduce the Please Role

- Remind yourself that you need to please God and you want to please some others.

- Practice how to say no in advance.

- Tell others directly what your objectives are and what you want.

- Give yourself sorting-out time each day to think through your priorities and plan activities.

- Every day, do something toward what you most want to accomplish in your lifetime and that fits your long-term lifestyle.

- Use a written action sheet or a to-do list during daily Time In.

Try Hard

People who play Try Hard roles often sigh and say, "I'll try..." They thrive on difficulty and talk about how hard they work. Frequently, they have two vertical lines etched between their eyebrows. Look into their early childhood programming, and you'll usually find a parent who constantly said, "Well, at least you tried. That's what counts."

Try Hards don't focus at the results of their time investment. They concentrate on getting an "A" for effort instead. They are often found in organizations that don't have clearly defined objectives. They get credit for trying hard, and they don't have to account for their failure to achieve the best results in the least amount of time. Good old Charlie may feel he deserves a lot of credit for burning the midnight oil on those progress reports. But if he needs results, he'd probably be a lot happier if he spent less time talking about the effort he's putting in. He might get the job done faster.

Finding easier ways to accomplish an objective does not detract from the quality of the result. Try hards don't focus on results. They feel that what counts is effort.

Trying hard is a way of operating, not an end in itself. Concentrating on effort rather than on results is limiting. First focus clearly on the results you want. You will free yourself to accomplish more in less time, without unnecessary effort. Work hard, but work on the right things.

Some Techniques to Reduce the Try Hard Role

- Clarify objectives before deciding upon activities.

- Give the right kind of time to the right things; find blocks of time for major jobs.

- Divide big projects into smaller, more workable units.

- Use gadgets such as recorders and calculators to multiply your time.

- Ask yourself every day, "What is an easier way to accomplish this?"

Be Strong

Traditional time techniques often work for the Be Strong type. These methods emphasize discipline and unemotional evaluation. That's meat and drink for the Be Strongs. They feel the only key to better time management is "more self-discipline." They don't believe in relying on anyone for help. They think it's just a question of adherence to stricter schedules. Be Strongs accomplish a lot, but they pay a price. They waste a lot of their time (and that of others) because they won't ask for help when it's appropriate to do so. They avoid any situation where they might appear weak.

Here's a typical demonstration of Be Strong behavior. A driver is looking for the right turnoff on the highway in an unfamiliar area. There's no map of the locality in the car, but he or she would never stop to ask for directions. Whether it's a salesman on the way to an important meeting or a den mother driving a minivan full of Cub Scouts, a Be Strong feels compelled to keep going no matter what—even if it wastes valuable time. Be Strongs rarely ask for help.

Some Techniques to Reduce the Be Strong Role

- Find opportunities to delegate more.

- Give yourself both Time In for productive action and Time Out for rest and relaxation.

- Set realistic deadlines for yourself and others.

- If you find yourself procrastinating, discover any feelings you are avoiding.

About All Five Roles

A few people respond to these concepts by saying, "I don't do any of those things!" Great. If that's accurate, you are operating from choice all the time. But that's not the case for most of us. Typically, we spend 50 to 90 percent of our time in compulsive roles. Even if you are the exception, it's helpful to understand how the rest of us operate.

(If you feel you need more information before you can make a decision about which ones you play, does the Be Perfect role sound familiar?)

Others respond by saying, "I do them all." Most of us do all of them at some time. Few of us do all of them at all times. Our time behavior changes and fluctuates as much as other aspects of our behavior and personality.

Don't be too quick to put an indelible label on yourself or anyone else. We can change. You play one role at one time and a different one at another time. Pick the two you play most frequently. You may use the same two roles on and off the job or they may differ in each situation.

What are your two major Compulsive Time roles?

At Work: Off the Job:

_____   _____

_____   _____

Based on your own experience and the techniques listed after each of the five types, pick two or three techniques that would be helpful for you to use more frequently.

At Work: Off the Job:

_____   _____

_____   _____

Help Others with Your Insights

When you understand your most frequent Compulsive Time uses, those around you can be more constructive in the ways they relate to you. I mentioned that I often let myself fall into the Hurry Up role when I'm under pressure. I typically combine that with a Be Strong mode. It's that old hurry-and-do-every-thing-yourself routine.

An associate has learned what to do when she sees me standing and working at my desk. She doesn't say, "You're into that Hurry Up, Be Strong mode." Instead, she reaches over, touches me lightly on the arm, and says, "Please sit down a moment. Tell me the most important thing I can do for you right now." It works every time. Why? First, the touch gets my attention. Normally I don't listen well when I'm hurrying. Sitting down also helps pull me out of the rushing mentality. Her emphasis on "most important" helps me set priorities. And her offer of assistance invites me out of the Be Strong role.

The Potential of Choice Time

When you operate from choice, you do your best thinking. You are free to explore the full range of alternatives open to you. You concentrate more fully on what you are doing. You can delve deeper into problems and uncover real causes.

Choice Time offers a special bonus in personal relationships. You can understand others more fully because you are not as preoccupied with how things are done. You will be giving people your full attention. And you'll enrich your time with your friends and family.

When we function from the blind spot of Compulsive Time use, we trap ourselves on the surface of problems. We don't get in touch with the deeper implications of the situation. When we operate from choice, we get below the superficial symptoms and discover the real issues and root causes. We solve the right problems. And we achieve better results.

The head of a construction company explained how an understanding of these issues improved his time use and his ability to make better decisions. "I used to rush around, always jumping from one problem to the next. I came up with some good solutions, but they weren't always the best. The long-range problems were never solved. I was too busy putting out brush fires to identify their causes.

"After I'd been exposed to the Choice Time concept, I realized how I'd been limiting myself. So I decided to take time away from the day-to-day rush, come in a hour early, and swim during lunch. Now there was more time to think about the larger issues and how to improve the company's overall profitability. One day in the pool, I realized that we could get a much better return on some assets if we divested one of our problem operations and invested the capital in long-term real estate holdings for development. By operating more from choice, I've made a strong improvement."

When you operate from Choice Time, you solve the right problems. You don't waste your time solving just any problems. The benefits are both organizational and personal. That's why it's worthwhile learning and implementing the techniques that will help reduce your Compulsive Time use. You will expand your Choice Time. You will get the best return on your time consistently.

Clear Your Mind with God's Truth

You have many ways to give yourself more clear-thinking Choice Time. My favorite is filling my mind with God's truth. Reading sections of the Bible, memorizing it, and praying through a quote from the Bible opens the way for more clear-thinking Choice Time.

> Jesus answered, "It is written: 'Man does not live on bread alone, but on every word that comes from the mouth of God'" (Matthew 4:4).

Key Points to Remember to Help You Conquer Compulsive Time Use

- Know which Compulsive Time roles you follow most frequently.

- Pick the time techniques that help reduce them.

- Concentrate on using those few time tools that reduce your Compulsive Time and expand your more productive Choice Time.

- Every day, clear the way to enjoy more of your creative and productive Choice Time.

- Clear your mind daily with God's truth.

Part III

Focusing Tools

For Direction and Organization

FOCUSING TOOLS

FOR DIRECTION
AND ORGANIZATION

- 🐚 Drop the pressure to get everything done.

- 🐚 Focus on the target of doing the right things at the right
  times.

Chapter 10

What to Carve Out When There's Too Much to Do

But seek first his kingdom and his righteousness, and all these things will be given to you as well.
Matthew 6:33

What's Ahead

- The plus of "productive selfishness."
- How two quick appointments can multiply your time.
- How a special time, a special place, and a special purpose add to your focus.

The warm pillow on a cold morning, the inviting music on the clock CD near the bed, and the pile of work after my days of travel helped me excuse sleepy tap after tap on the snooze button until the doorbell jolted me upright. The slap of reality reminded me that this was the morning that a dear friend had driven across town at the crack of dawn to see me before we both started to work.

Even though my forgiving friend helped dispel some of the discomfort of a meeting with clothes pulled on a body without a shower and a face without makeup, the late start and hurried morning was like a line of upright dominos starting to fall. As soon as she walked out the door, my quick shower, dressing, and rushing to get to work didn't stop the collapse of dominos during the morning. When I picked up the phone at 11:15, I was told, "You were scheduled to be in the dental hygienist's office at 11 A.M. Since we didn't get a cancellation call 24 hours in advance, we'll bill you." The voice continued to inform me that the first time I could be rescheduled was six weeks later. As I hung up the phone, a reality shouted through my mind: I need to spend time with God and spend time planning.

Carve Out Time for Two Appointments

Time is less pressured and moves more smoothly when you carve out time for two quick appointments each day. First, an appointment with God for wisdom and strength. Second, an appointment with yourself for planning, problem solving, and celebration.

This is true whether you're traveling or in town. It's true even though the appointments take only 15 minutes or so. In the rush of my travel and return, I had not carved out that time. I had fallen into bed without my usual appointment with myself to study my calendar and line up commitments for the next day.

Saying that I didn't have time was true, but the disorderly consequences took more time than a 15-minute appointment and cost more money than was necessary. Time dedicated to planning and organizing hands you the delights of more order, better results, and less chaos.

Another may find it easy to say, "I have too many interruptions." Consider the number of interruptions many people face from family, friends, and associates. Add in email beeping on your computer, phones ringing, pagers vibrating, cell phones buzzing, and faxes landing on your desk. Carving out a few minutes to anticipate problems will hand you back much more time in prevented problems.

"I'm too tired," might be the response of another person. These widespread feelings of fatigue must be respected. In these cases, give extra care to trading time on nonessentials for time on sleep, exercise, and planning for a more satisfying lifestyle. Once the process of carving out the two appointments gets underway—even if they are very short—you will find more ways to focus your time and have more time for needed rest.

Whenever I'm tempted to question, "But there is too much I have to do," the truth that Jesus spoke provides the perfect answer:

> I am the vine, you are the branches; he who abides in
> Me and I in him, he bears much fruit, for apart from Me
> you can do nothing (John 15:5 NASB).

Another question is, "What if the day is already chaotic and the dominos have already started to tumble?" The classic comment of "better late than never" works here. After the call about the missed dental appointment, what needed to be done was clear. Get up and walk away from my work, sit on a quiet step, open my Bible, read a couple of favorite paragraphs, then pray and ask for God's help in putting the to-do items on my calendar back in order. If you hesitate asking for God's help repeatedly, King David's example encourages us:

> David inquired of God again (1 Chronicles 14:14).

The person who feels too pressured to carve out those two appointments—one with God and one with yourself—often needs to turn on extra creativity to find some time that will work. It may be the middle of an afternoon lull while you are at your desk. It may be changing time typically spent sitting with the newspaper into time spent with your Bible, calendar, and organizer. It may be waiting for a child to finish soccer practice and spreading out your materials on the car seat as you wait. It may be dedicating time on a bus commute to work concentrating on these two appointments. Or it may be going to a nearby coffee shop and sitting at a quiet table with a cup of steaming brew.

Whatever the complications, most of us have heard that it makes sense to carve out time with God for wisdom and perspective and carve out time with ourselves for focusing, problem solving, and problem preventing.

Special Time, Special Place

The following quick tips can help you find your own way to enjoy the benefits of both of these types of appointments. Few people have this time automatically open in their daily lives. For most, this quiet time must be deliberately carved out of an already packed schedule. A great way to do this is to make appointments with yourself. Appointments give importance and call for respect. When you explain to someone, "I have an appointment at 7:00," few people argue. Why not transfer that benefit to your appointment with God and your appointment with yourself?

Some people will stand in front of you and insist that the only time to have these appointments is the first thing in the morning, and that is time I hear about most frequently. It has a large number of pluses, but don't feel guilty if you have your appointment with God in the evening. You may be like busy Nicole, who feels extra energy start flowing in the evening. So she has carved out time away from her husband and grandmother at 9 P.M. when she sits at the end of the divan in their little-used living room with a pillow on her lap for a table. She combines her two appointments, although many people have them at separate times.

You gain two big benefits when you find a special place. First, you condition yourself to start your appointment the moment you get there. Second, you eliminate the distractions of your usual reading or workplace. Sonya gets up 30 minutes before her family awakens and sits at the end of the counter in their family room with her Bible and organizer in front of her. Tim pulls a stool up to his workbench in the garage at 7:00 in the evening with his Bible open. One woman from a family of five children remembers her father's special place in their busy house in the country was a chair in the basement pulled next to the warmth of the water heater. Another woman remembers her childhood comfort of peeking around the half-closed door any evening at 8:00 and seeing her mother lying across her bed with her Bible open in front of her.

While a special place is not essential, it is very helpful for most. If you struggle with having a regular appointment with God or a regular appointment with yourself, find a special place.

In Your Appointment with God

Let's look at three simple tips for having an enriching appointment with God:

1. Listen to God in the Bible

If you are just starting to read the Bible, turn to the table of contents and mark these six great places to read: Matthew, Mark, Luke, John, Psalms, and Proverbs. After you open your Bible, ask God to show you what He wants you to learn and do as a result of your reading. Also ask Him to help you understand more of His character.

2. Talk to God in prayer

When my friend Elizabeth Paeth Lasker encouraged me to talk with God in prayer and ask Him for whatever I wanted, that was a new concept. Before that time, talking with God had been reserved for lost luggage and earthquakes. Yet as I read the Bible, His character showed care for individuals and concern about details, like numbering the hairs on my head and noticing the fall of a tiny sparrow. Not just the fall of a majestic eagle. The fall of a sparrow! That told me God cared about the everyday details in my life.

But I still brought a bad habit to the appointment. Passivity. I longed for others—including God—to guess what I needed and give it to me without my asking. The Bible, however, presents a different strategy: Ask for what you want.

Jesus even asked a blind man what he wanted:

> And Jesus stopped and commanded that he be brought to Him; and when he had come near, He questioned him, "What do you want Me to do for you?" And he said, "Lord, I want to regain my sight!" And Jesus said to him, "Receive your sight; your faith has made you well" (Luke 18:40-42 NASB).

In the next example of Jesus teaching the multitudes, Jesus gives a surprising instruction in the last two words:

> If you then, being evil, know how to give good gifts to your children, how much more will your Father who is in heaven give what is good to those who ask Him! (Matthew 7:11 NASB).

If you are saying that asking God for what you want sounds selfish, Jesus gives us the next part: asking directly and also confirming clearly that you want the will of God the Father. He models this for us in this prayer in the Garden of Gethsemane:

> My Father, if it is possible, may this cup be taken from me. Yet not as I will, but as you will (Matthew 26:39).

The process is clear. Ask God. Ask about anything. And also confirm that you want His will.

3. Apply

Many times when you read the Bible and pray, a specific item of action will come to your mind. Perhaps asking someone for forgiveness, praying for a friend who is ill, giving a gift to your church or a missionary. If the action you are prompted to take follows biblical principles, do it now. (If something comes to your mind that does not follow biblical principles, like "rob a bank," you can drop that idea in the wastebasket.)

The three key actions of listening to God in the Bible, talking with God in prayer, and applying what He is showing you makes sense. They make a difference. And they help you think and act more clearly.

In Your Appointment with Yourself

In these few minutes each day, think about what really counts. Concentrate on the things that will last. Think about the purpose and mission for your life. Think about what will make the difference in your life, your work, and the lives of the people around you for the long term. Then see in your mind these long-term results completed. Picture in faith what you are working toward.

Why does this process pay such rich dividends? When you are rushed, rattled, or pressured, it is difficult to think above day-to-day demands or think strategically. It's like having your nose pressed against a painting. It is hard to see how things fit together. When you have a clear focus on the big picture, you have more motivation to work through the tough times. When you hold the long-term in mind, you make better day-to-day decisions. You stay out of blind alleys. You know what is the most important thing to do next. When you glimpse the top of the mountain, you gain the energy for the climb under your feet. Here are some ways to prepare yourself.

1. Calm your mind

If you have had your appointment with God immediately before you have your appointment with yourself, your mind will probably be calm and clear. However, if your schedule and style leads you to have the two appointments at different times, here's a great way to calm your mind.

Take some small Post-it Notes and capture all the thoughts that are buzzing around in your head. Write a couple of words for each thought on one Post-it Note. Don't worry about order or duplication at this time. (You'll see more details on this system later in this chapter.) Writing them down calms most people. It lets your mind know that you won't forget an item. After you have put them down, ask God for His guidance and start grouping them. Things that have to be done today go on your calendar sheet for today. Things that have to be done tomorrow, on the calendar for tomorrow. Some people enter the items directly on the right day in their personal digital assistant. Others use a low-tech binder. The focus is not on one type of organizer or calendar. It is on using what works for you to help you calm and collect your thoughts.

2. Think back—Where did your time go?

Too often people forget this point and fall into the time waste of making the same mistakes again and again. As you think back over your time, exactly where did your time go? What did you accomplish? Where did you run into problems? How long did things take? What lessons did you learn?

3. Think ahead—Focus your targets and prevent problems

Think about where you want to go and your specific targets. If you haven't set specific targets for yourself, you shortchange yourself. It's too easy to be busy doing things that don't really count for yourself or others.

If you have ever stood in the middle of a situation and said to yourself, "I knew this was going to happen," you are reminding yourself of how clearly we can often predict problems. Your appointment with yourself is a great time to anticipate and then prevent problems. Remind yourself: "I can think for myself. I can solve problems. I can decide. And I can do new things."

Here are three examples to help you fine-tune a practice that works for you. Bob pulls his stack of 3 x 5 cards with questions from a desk drawer and props one against the penholder on his desk at work. Then he concentrates and makes notes. One card he uses has three questions he copied from a Peter F. Drucker book:

1. What is our business?

2. Who is our customer?

3. What does the customer value?

Elizabeth gets up early for some quiet moments at her kitchen table before she talks to her husband, children, or any of the doctors and nurses who report to her. Brian still settles into the couch when the children are asleep, but he no longer switches on the television for a look at the evening news. Now he grabs his organizer notebook, replays in his mind his mental pictures of where he wants to go, and then takes pencil to paper with specific plans to get there.

4. Celebrate

You may say you don't have time to celebrate your accomplishments, but giving yourself a pat on the back puts energy into your time. It also helps you know what to do more of next time.

5. List next steps

Before you start deciding what you need to do, ask for God's help and guidance. As you write action steps, divide them into the size that will motivate you. For example, some people can write on their calendar "Call Bob Smith and get an order" and that's enough. Another person may need smaller motivational steps and write "Plan Bob Smith call," and then write another step with "Make Bob Smith call and get an order." Put your action steps into the size of motivational units that encourage you to do them and cross them out.

Here's an example of how the right-sized motivational unit helps. At one time if you were to thumb through my calendar for the previous six months, you would not have seen one minute of exercise. And every day of delay made starting more daunting until I found a form that allowed me to put an "X" in the block for each five minutes of exercise. It worked for me. Do what it takes to motivate you.

Lining up what you are going to do gives you energy. It helps you concentrate. It motivates you. If you are sitting down as you plan, you may have a hard time keeping your seat on the chair. You are so ready for action.

Carry and Use an Organizer That Fits Your Style

Although people will argue about which calendar/organizer works best, use something. If you have to buy three or four to find the one that works for you, do it. Or put your own system together. Organizers don't box you in as many people fear. They free you. They can help you relax more fully and avoid worry. They boost your ability to concentrate and to recover from interruptions.

If you don't jot down an upcoming appointment, you'll keep reminding yourself of it again and again. A reminder about a dental appointment will float to the surface of your mind when you are trying to concentrate on writing a report. Worry that you'll forget an item for a meeting can dampen your fun in a movie. A nagging feeling that you may have missed a friend's birthday can interfere with the free flow of ideas you need in an interview.

Develop the habit of looking at your calendar regularly to stay up-to-date with your commitments, and you won't find commitments intruding haphazardly on your concentration. This will help you give yourself time off when you want it. Check to see if you are giving yourself the right amount of relaxing, nonproductive Time Out as well. Schedule the right amount of stimulation and excitement for your needs. Study your calendar and deliberately design your time.

Review your calendar whenever you otherwise would be wasting time waiting. When someone puts you on hold on the telephone, use those few minutes to study your calendar. If you must wait for an appointment, open your calendar.

Get used to looking at your calendar frequently. It will be easier to remember to write down your commitments when you make them. If you promise to phone someone in three weeks, write the commitment in your calendar as soon as you make the promise. Then you won't have to think about it again until you have to make the call.

If you accept a dinner invitation, write the date, time, and place in your calendar. If necessary, get the map or print the directions on how to get there. Make a note to pick up a hospitality gift.

Don't Be Afraid of a To-Do List

Writing out a daily list of things to do in priority order is another major time-saving technique, but it sets up a lot of resistance among many people. Usually it's that old fear of being boxed in. Sometimes, it's a deep-seated reaction to the authoritarian sound of "to do." In reality, these lists can help you develop the technique of finishing fully. Completing the tasks listed on such a sheet can create energizing feelings of accomplishment. For these reasons, it's worthwhile overcoming any resistance you might feel.

If you write to-do lists but lose them, change the title. Call it an action sheet or a wrap-up list. Find a title that appeals to you. If your old habit for a day off is to write a 20-item to-do list, lose it, and then curl up with a murder mystery, write a special list. Motivate yourself by sprinkling a variety of tempting activities throughout your list.

Sticky Notes to Get Things off Your Mind and into Your Priorities

When I am feeling the stress of juggling a number of things in my mind, I know it's calendar time. Remember those Post-it Notes we discussed earlier? I sit at a table and write a few words on a yellow sticky note about each concern I have been juggling. One idea or task to one note. Sometimes the area of the table in front of me is covered with notes, but most of the time only five or six are spread out on the table.

Something happens when I do this. My mind calms. My concentration grows. My focus sharpens. Then I move each sticky note into groups of related items. Put the most important or urgent items at the top of the collection. Pull out the items that need to be done today and this week. Then I put each note on the page in my organizer when I am going to do it or on the project plan where it relates. A note about "buy XYZ" goes into my organizer divider for shopping. Now I have an action sheet made of up sticky notes to focus me during the day.

If you need extra motivation, add any implements that will help your time program work smoothly—special pens, colored stickers, a desk that helps you feel orderly. Anything that helps motivate you to get going and keep going in the right direction or adds to the pleasure of the time you invest is worth using.

Building Something Big and Beautiful

Here's a plus to the process. Building contractor Jack gave a special insight into the power of writing action steps when he pointed to a big and beautiful building that his company had constructed. "It's simple," he concluded, as he looked at the expanse of windows soaring upward and reflecting the sunlight, "Write the steps. Pray the steps. Do the steps."

How true. And how transferable. You can use Jack's system to build something big and beautiful in your life. Write the steps. Pray the steps. Do the steps.

Carving out the two appointments during the day gives you more time, more focus, and more power. Giving yourself the two appointments each day doesn't mean you can't ever reach for the snooze button or enjoy an extra few minutes with your head burrowed into a warm pillow on a cold morning. However it does mean that you will give your days the warm security of less pressure.

Big Idea and Quick Tips

Cut the chaos. Reduce the pressure. And get more of the right things done by finding some time for two appointments. Give yourself a head start with a special time and a special place for each one.

During your appointment with God:

- Listen to God in the Bible.

- Talk to God in prayer about anything on your heart.

- Ask God to help you know how to apply what you are reading. Then act on it.

During your appointment with yourself:

- Calm yourself. Move buzzing ideas from your mind to your organizer.

- Think back—where did your time go?

- Think ahead—focus on your targets, the right things to be doing, and the problems that need to be solved or prevented.

- Celebrate. Thank God for your accomplishments and give yourself the encouragement of a pat on the back.

- Decide your next steps.

Remember the key. It's not how long you spend, it's how faithful and consistent you are. The value comes from finding even a few quick moments each day for perspective and planning. Do it daily. Have this plan ready and you will have a head start even when people complicate your time.

Chapter 11

What to Put in When People Pull You off Target

But I tell you: Love your enemies and pray for those who persecute you, that you may be sons of your Father in heaven.
Matthew 5:44,45

What's Ahead

• Why good processes are worth up-front time.

• What to do when other people cause your time problems.

• How to cut time-draining stress with "Fix the process and not the person."

Three reasons stand behind this chapter on the value of putting the right processes in place early in the game. In addition, you'll see the benefits of fixing the process early in any problem.

The first reason is that although most books on time emphasize setting goals and knowing exactly what you want to accomplish as the first thing to do, as I have studied the Bible, I have seen a greater emphasis placed on good processes first. How you do things. General reasons *why* you do things. Less on specific objectives first. There is no scene where Jesus sits down with Peter, James, and John and tells them to formulate exact quarterly goals. However, there are many examples of what to do and reasons why to do it rather than the spotlight being on exactly what you want to accomplish. Consider three scenes where Jesus tells people how to live and what processes to follow:

> For if you forgive men their trespasses, your heavenly Father will also forgive you. But if you do not forgive men their trespasses, neither will your Father forgive your trespasses (Matthew 6:14,15 NKJV).

> Judge not, that you be not judged. For with what judgment you judge, you will be judged; and with the measure you use, it will be measured back to you (Matthew 7:1,2 NKJV).

> Ask, and it will be given to you; seek, and you will find; knock, and it will be opened to you. For everyone who asks receives, and he who seeks finds, and to him who knocks it will be opened (Matthew 7:7,8 NKJV).

The second reason is that people tell me they don't set objectives and targets because people complicate their lives, particularly difficult people. And a great solution for people complications is fixing the process and not the person. For example, think what could happen if everyone adopted the process of praying first when faced with a difficult person.

The third reason is that in studying effective, successful, and happy people, many of them do not have written goals. However, they all have good processes. They serve others, work diligently, and use good stewardship in caring for their resources. They know about fixing the process.

So that's why this chapter on the importance of good processes comes before the also-important chapters on knowing what you want and defining your objectives. Good targets and objectives are important, but good processes come first.

When Others Cause Your Problems

This is a reality few are taught. This reality strikes me often as I tailor seminars for organizations I serve. As we survey and call people before the seminars to learn their specific challenges, one question consistently crops up.

"What if your problems are caused by other people?"

The answer is practical: The place to start is the process.

The words "process" and "processes" have a number of definitions. Here's a practical one from the dictionary: "a series of actions or operations directed toward a result." Or you may want a more detailed definition: a collection of activities that takes one or more kinds of input to produce an output that is of greater value. Or you can use this streamlined definition of a process: a good habit with a good purpose.

Whether you use the word "process" or "processes," the response is the same. Pay attention to them more than ever before.

When you consistently treat everyone in right ways, you are using right processes. When you do, you build confidence. You build relationships. You certainly save time.

"Okay," you say, "I see some time saving. But where are the major time savings from paying attention to process?" You enjoy big benefits because keeping a spotlight on processes clears out three wastes: complaining, blaming, and criticizing.

Check your experience. Haven't you seen tremendous time wasted when people blame others—or themselves—rather than solving the problem?

The following examples of "fix the process and not the person" are designed to persuade you and stimulate your thinking—to make "fixing the process and not the person" one of the first tools you reach for.

When People Complicate Your Time, the First Tool to Reach for—Fix the Process, Not the Person

This example shows what Brad did when people complicated his time at home. Brad felt irritated when he walked down the hall by the bathroom his children used. It bothered his orderly nature to see bath towels wadded and slung across the towel bars. But towel arrangement was such a small item compared to the other things on his agenda for his children, he decided not to spend any more time nagging. Instead he took down the towel bars and installed a row of towel hooks. Problem solved. Fix the process and not the person.

Right processes prevent wasting time on nagging and criticism of others or yourself. It is always a better use of your time to fix the process rather than trying to fix the person.

The Process of Speaking the Truth in Love

Stacey works with a man in the next cubical who interrupts her. Not once a day. Not twice a day. Twice an hour. Stacey's associate says he doesn't like to read the manuals. "Tutorials take too much time." He would rather sit at his computer and try to figure out each new application on his own. When he can't, he says it is so much faster to ask Stacey.

Stacey does have the banner hanging over her cubical that reads "CTC" for Computer Technical Coordinator. She did receive the extra training on new applications. She did volunteer for the unpaid coordinator role. And she did tell her associates she would be happy to help them.

But now Stacey feels frustrated. One of her team members left last week, and she has shouldered part of his responsibilities too. Stacey tells herself that her associate with all the questions should know about her workload. He should know he isn't the only person she helps. He should know how hard it is to concentrate with an interruption every ten minutes.

But Stacey does not put the irritation she feels into words. Finally one Thursday afternoon, Stacey gets one more interruption. It's the same question he asked two days ago. And again yesterday. This time Stacey explodes. She tells him that he is inconsiderate. Selfish. Slow. Shouldn't be working for a high-tech company if he can't handle the technology.

That night Stacey is in turmoil. She spends dinner with her husband explaining all the details. Even after dinner, she replays in her mind what she said. What he said. What she should have said.

The next morning, as Stacey is praying and reading her Bible, she remembers something she had read. Words that would have saved her stress, time, frustration, and friendship: Speak the truth in love (Ephesians 4:15).

So Stacey rehearses and then spends the first few minutes at work with her interrupter. She listens to his viewpoint. She describes hers. She says what she feels. She asks for what she wants. She clears the air. And she gets closure. Now Stacey is the first one to cheer for the powerful process of "speak the truth in love."

A Process to Save Everyone Time

In this example of "fix the process and not the people," Edna used to blame and complain about the waiters and waitresses on her shift. No matter how many times she told them, they forgot to ask customers at the restaurant if they wanted a beverage and dessert. Those two items spelled profit, and the crew members on her shift still forgot.

Edna decided to "fix the system and not the person." She stopped nagging. She stopped complaining about "employees nowadays." She started putting informal graphs on the wall in the hall near the kitchen. She started charting two totals for each shift: Number of beverages served and number of desserts served. Simple line graphs showed the daily numbers.

Then things started changing. Crew members started looking at the charts. They started asking how the first shift sold twice as many desserts as they did. They started talking to each other. And, most of all, they started serving more beverages and desserts. This example spotlights the lesson. Don't spend your time trying to change others. Fix the process so you can help them do their best.

Prevent Blaming Yourself

Milton used to scold himself for forgetting to take his medicine. His doctor had warned him of the dangers of stroke if he forgot his medications. But he still was so busy he forgot on some days. So Milton bought a small plastic box with seven compartments—one for each day of the week. On Saturday he sorts his medications for the week into his "medicine minder," puts it next to the kitchen sink, and relaxes. He doesn't need to fix or blame himself because he has fixed the process.

Cutting the Complaining and Blaming with a Television Process

Here's another example. Sharon used to shudder when she thought of her job as training director during the summer at her social service agency. It meant teenagers. It meant a crowd. And it meant training teens who had never held jobs before, who had spent most of their time on the street, and who had not been taught personal hygiene and habits for work. As training director for the downtown center of her agency, summer also meant she got complaints from the other side. She fielded frustrations from line managers about long stays in the rest room, bare midriffs, and body odor.

This afternoon, Sharon sat in the back of the room watching the nurse give a presentation on hygiene and dress for work while 20 teenagers talked and shoved each other. When the nurse raised her voice to an even louder level to get people's attention, Sharon came to a conclusion.

No more trying to fix the teenagers. No more blaming the nurse. No more blaming herself. She was reminded that she was working with the television generation. So she videotaped the nurse giving the same presentation. Then she brought in the next group of teens plus TV monitors for an experiment. This time, as she played the video on the television, there was no talking or shoving. Sharon was amazed to see this group of teenagers quietly watching the same nurse on TV. It was the same message, but a new process.

A Process for the Five-Hour Drive

You have probably experienced your version of this stressful example and the need for healing in strained family relationships.

As Gary and I walked through the door, he almost bounced with enthusiasm about how one process had helped him with painful time pressures. He smiled and continued, "If we were to stand here until tomorrow morning, I would not run out of examples of how this one idea has helped me." He went on to explain that he had no trouble telling his friends and people at work no. But when it came to family members, his "yes" switch was on too often and his stress mounted.

Gary said that last week the stress started as he stood near the kitchen counter and finished taking phone messages. His stomach had tied itself into knots. For years his wife's parents had insisted that Gary and his wife ride with them to family weddings or funerals that were often across the state. Although his wife's father couldn't physically drive because of a heart condition, he still tried to drive from the passenger seat. These four-and five-hour rides several times a year would be filled with a moment-by-moment stream of commands and reprimands to his wife: "Pass that truck." "Why did you pull into this lane?" "That was stupid." "You're going too slow." "Watch your speed." His onslaught of comments could make a five-hour drive seem like a ten-hour trek to Gary and his wife as they sat in the backseat. The last trip together was so frustrating that Gary munched his way through an entire bag of potato chips during the trip, and he and his wife ended up snapping at each other for no reason during the next two days.

Now with the call about an uncle's funeral at the end of the week, he was feeling again the pressure for another ride with painful togetherness. His wife's parents had brushed away previous requests for new conversation and offers to drive, so this time Gary and his wife prayed, asked Jesus what would please Him, and then decided to put these long rides on their List of Lessons Learned. Now, no matter how much his wife's father jabs with, "What's the matter with you? You like to waste gas?" and insists that they ride together, Gary and his wife are firm. They appreciate the offer but are more comfortable taking their own car.

When you have had a stressful time, think about it. Pray about it. Consider what the Bible says about it. Then try to fix the process and not the person. Using the right process reduces time-wasting stress, and it gives you more opportunities to find time.

The Right Process to Help Your Time

For a customer satisfaction manager, a right process might be getting ongoing feedback from customers.

For a manufacturing manager, a process might be spending one hour each day walking around the plant. Looking. Asking. Listening.

For a person in direct sales, it might be scheduling five qualified interviews a day.

For a father, a right process might be looking into the eyes of each of his children every day and saying, "I love you."

The process of enhancing our time is not without complications. Most of us can't closet ourselves for hours of uninterrupted planning. Most of us can't assume there will be no interruptions, no breakdowns, no emergencies, and no difficult people. Most of us can't ignore people and don't want to. So when you face challenges, first fix the process and not the person.

Chapter 12

Turning True Wants into Practical Targets

An intelligent person aims at wise action,
but a fool starts off in many directions.
Proverbs 17:24 TEV

What's Ahead?

- The surprising question that Jesus asked and how it can help your time.
- Three big questions that can help you move ahead.
- How practical targets help you say no to the good and yes to the best.

Many of us don't set objectives or write targets even though we have heard of their importance. Some people have heard that it doesn't please God to know what you want or to have targets. They haven't been shown the number of quotes in the Bible in which Jesus actually asks people what they want.

> Jesus stopped and called them, and said, "What do you want Me to do for you?" (Matthew 20:32 NASB).

Jesus also asked His close disciples what they wanted. Even when they wanted something that was off target, He didn't correct them for wanting. He corrected them for *what* they wanted:

> James and John, the two sons of Zebedee, came up to Jesus, saying, "Teacher, we want You to do for us whatever we ask of You." And He said to them, "What do you want Me to do for you?" They said to Him, "Grant that we may sit, one on Your right and one on Your left, in Your glory." But Jesus said to them, "You do not know what you are asking. Are you able to drink the cup that I drink, or to be baptized with the baptism with which I am baptized?" (Mark 10:35-38 NASB).

People who say that knowing what you want displeases God do not consider that the apostle Paul told people that though he wanted to travel to certain destinations, he also prayed for God's guidance and accepted new objectives. They don't see the difference between having an objective and rigidly grasping an objective no matter what God prompts.

For many people, the problem of not knowing what they want often stems from early childhood programming.

When you were a child, did you hear, "You don't know what you want" or "I'll tell you what you want" or even, "What you want is…"? This type of conditioning can carry over into adult life. It's easy to grow up with the feeling that someone else has to tell you what you want because you can't think for yourself. The reality is that you can think for yourself. In fact, you can think clearly about anything. (Of course, some things might not be worth thinking about.)

You may hold yourself back from knowing what you want because you think your objective must be perfect. It doesn't. You can change your mind. As you update your wants continually throughout your life, you may find that they have changed because your circumstances and maturity have changed.

There's also a widespread myth that knowing what you want is synonymous with being pushy, rude, or egotistical. Listen to the tone of voice most people use when they say something like, "She really knows what she wants." You will often hear an undertone of disapproval.

The truth is that knowing what you want is a preliminary step to setting meaningful targets or objectives. Here's an easy way to begin.

The Wants Inventory

The Wants Inventory technique allows you to use what you don't want to help you uncover what you do want.

Turn to a fresh sheet in your Time Notebook and make two columns: What I Think God Wants More of in My Life and What God Wants Less Of. When you have been praying and reading the Bible daily and listening to messages based on the Bible, you will have items for this page.

Here is a prayer that will help you complete your Wants Inventory:

> Dear God, I want to please You. I know that the only things
> that will satisfy me and give me joy are what You want for
> me. Please give me clear direction about what You want more
> of and less of in my time.

But don't wait for God to drop a picnic basket into your lap with a printed, detailed plan inside. Follow God's principles and keep on defining your direction as you ask for His guidance.

Now turn to a fresh sheet in your Time Notebook and make two more columns: What I Want More Of and What I Want Less Of. Before you begin making a list, consider your life as a whole. Think in terms of work and recreation, business and personal life. Include ideas that relate to accomplishments and lifestyle.

Begin with your Want More Of list if you can. If you feel stymied, write something in the Less Of column. Then, take a good look at it and see if the flip side can provide a key to something you can list under More Of. For instance, you may want to spend fewer vacations sitting around in your own backyard. This could translate to the More Of column as "traveling to Europe," "camping in the Rockies," "a trip to the Grand Canyon," "time at Disneyland," "a sailboat," or "golf clubs."

Each time you list something under Less Of, balance it with something under More Of. Continue until you have 20 items listed in the More Of column.

Now look over the items in the More Of column and circle those that you want most. This helps clarify and update what is really central to your life.

Make a new Wants Inventory in your notebook every day for one week. Don't refer to a previous list until you have completed your new day's list. Then compare it with the items that appear on the other lists. Which items appear only once? Which recur? Are you circling the same "want most" items every day?

Use this technique on a weekly or monthly basis to update your wants. It's an effective way to begin setting all kinds of objectives. Short-term objectives are easier. Long-range objectives are more important. Concentrate on discovering these first by working backwards. Identify what you most want to accomplish in life and what you want your long-range lifestyle to be. Then work backwards to discover the steps that will lead to your ultimate destination.

The following surefire techniques have helped thousands set meaningful objectives.

Three Big Questions

First, answer three questions:

1. Who are the people you serve? No one is in isolation. Our happiness and success depend on serving people. Define who they are for you at this point in your life.

2. What do you most want to accomplish in your lifetime?

3. What do you want your long-term lifestyle to be?

For example, here are some possible answers:

Accomplishments

- Build a house
- Rear two children with good character so they have happy, satisfying, and productive lives
- Be financially secure
- Help the people you love trust Jesus Christ
- Visit every major league ballpark in the United States
- Sail to the South Pacific
- Become president of the company

- Found a successful business
- Become a millionaire
- Teach a Bible study
- Start a shelter for battered women and children
- Compose a symphony
- Become an expert bridge player
- Get a degree

Lifestyle

- Live in the country
- Be able to walk to work and church
- Be your own boss
- Live alone
- Have people in your home frequently for birthday parties and celebrations
- Be married
- Travel frequently
- Have daily contact with competent and caring people
- Live near the ocean
- Live in a 30-story penthouse

No one else can answer these questions for you. So spend a quiet, uninterrupted 15 minutes considering them. Select a blank page in your Time Notebook and write out your answers. Be specific; your progress will be easier because you'll have a sharp focus on what you want. You will be surprised and delighted by the amount of information you will discover.

Make sure you have balance in your Wants Inventory. If everything is an arrow pointed inward, your direction won't satisfy you. Make sure you have arrows pointing outward in service to others.

> Remembering the words that the Lord Jesus himself said, "There is more happiness in giving than in receiving" (Acts 20:35 TEV).

Allison knew the way to happiness is to focus on reaching out to others in service, but she wasn't sure she had taught this to her children. As she backed her minivan out of the parking lot after an enrichment session with other homeschooling families, Allison thought how much she loved the squirming bunch of kids buckled into the back seats. She found herself praying that they could learn more of the joy of reaching out to others. At home that night, she prayed with her husband as they went to bed.

Later that week when she was again in their minivan with the kids buckled in back, and as she turned the corner near a convalescent hospital, the answer danced into her mind. But then she thought of all the complications. Money. Time. Not the usual things for kids to want to do.

However, some months later she stood at the back of the dining room at the convalescent hospital and smiled with joy as she saw the excitement that only preteen kids can have. The room was still as three of her children presented a puppet show for a room full of hospital residents. As the songs from the tape recorder praised God with a Jamaican beat, and as the puppets popping over the low curtain "sang" and swayed, she saw one of the long-term residents tapping her gnarled fingers on the front of her wheelchair and tears coming to her eyes as she heard about the love of Jesus for each of us.

Designing your daily efforts to contribute to what you value most makes your time satisfying. Doing something daily toward your lifetime accomplishments and lifestyle adds meaning. Doing something daily that serves others adds joy. Do it daily and feel great.

Review and rewrite your answers to these Wants Inventory questions periodically, depending on your personal situation. Many successful people spend one or two minutes reviewing their lifetime accomplishments and lifestyle each day. This helps them keep these ideas fresh in their minds. A sales executive revolutionized his sales volume by rewriting his answers on the front of his monthly calendar. He doesn't always change his answers, but writing them out each month etches the ideas more deeply into his consciousness. Others do it when they pay bills, or on birthdays, or on holidays.

The One Hundredth Birthday Technique

This technique can provide a useful perspective on long-range accomplishments. Imagine that you are being interviewed by a newspaper reporter on your one hundredth birthday and asked to name your most important accomplishments. How would you like to answer this question? Be specific. Would you like to say you'd started a successful charitable foundation? Made a million dollars? Written a bestseller? Become an astronaut? Reared two healthy children?

Here's an illustration of how one woman used the one hundredth birthday idea to solve a dilemma concerning her short-term objectives.

Susan had run a special camp for handicapped kids for three summers that involved about 300 hours of work yearly. She loved the work even though the pay was minimal. Now the camp's board of directors was pressing her to continue for another year.

Susan also wanted to have a baby, continue her studies for an MBA, and help her husband landscape their yard. She found herself in a spin of questions about what to do. Should she take the camp job for another summer? It was such a good cause. Should she delay her MBA studies? Should they wait to have a baby? What about the landscaping? Then Susan took time to consider these questions in light of her one hundredth birthday. What did she want her lifestyle to be like then? What accomplishments did she want to be able to point to? She realized that she most wanted to be surrounded by family. She also wanted that MBA. So she resigned as camp director and opted for the things that were most important to her. Knowing her long-range desires made her short-term decisions easier.

The Security of Short-Term Objectives

A clear understanding of what you most want to accomplish in the long run pays off years before your one hundredth birthday. You will be in a good position to set specific short-term objectives that provide security in the day-to-day rush and keep you on the right path. You will be in touch with your ultimate destination and gain confidence and satisfaction because you are moving toward what matters most.

Use your Time Notebook to help clarify your short-term objectives. Write out specific answers to these questions:

Five years from now, what do you want your work life to be like?

- What do you want your job title to be?
- Where do you want to be working?
- What do you want your annual salary to be?
- What associations do you want to belong to?
- What awards do you want to earn?

Five years from now, what do you want your personal life to be like?

- What do you want in terms of family and friends?
- What do you want to look like?
- What skills and educational accomplishments do you want to have?
- What do you want your net worth to be?
- What do you want to weigh?

When you've answered these questions, repeat the process with a one-year time frame. How well do your one-year objectives relate to your five-year objectives?

Short-term objectives can range from five years to 15 minutes. You may be feeling so pressured that you can only think in terms of getting through the day. Sometimes a person's energy level is so low, the best thing is a 15-minute objective: "I won't eat any candy for the next 15 minutes." "Fifteen minutes from now, I will have written the first paragraph of that report." It's okay to set the same goal at the end of the next 15 minutes.

The What-I-Want-to-Happen Memo

The What-I-Want-to-Happen memo is another helpful way to use short-term objectives. An investment adviser used this technique to increase her sales performance. She used to arrive for initial interviews with a briefcase bulging with every possible investment opportunity. But she often went away without a check in her hand, and she became increasingly frustrated. Now she composes a WIWTH memo before she goes into a meeting, writing out specifically what she wants to happen. "What I want from this meeting is for you to say that you want me to help you achieve financial freedom. And I want to have a firm appointment within two weeks to present three specific investment opportunities most suited to you."

The WIWTH memo also can help you relax more fully. Many people feel guilty if they aren't always productive, and that guilt can block their enjoyment of leisure activities. One man used the WIWTH technique to get himself off the guilt hook he'd created during his occasional Saturday fishing trips. His enjoyment of his friends and the fishing used to be marred by guilt feelings. He would worry about the chores he'd left undone at home and the paperwork still on his desk. Now before each trip, he reminds himself of what he wants to happen: "What I want from this time is to enjoy being with friends and have fun fishing." As he steps off the gangplank at the end of the day, he feels good. He's achieved his objective. The old guilt is gone. He enjoyed himself even though the lawn needs mowing.

Enjoy more focus. Pick two or three upcoming events in your life and write a WIWTH memo for each one.

Update Wants and Objectives

Finding out what you most want and setting objectives isn't a one-time exercise. It's an ongoing process. To get the best return on your time, make it a habit to renew the answers to the questions in this chapter and continually update your long-term objectives.

It's particularly valuable to review and rewrite your answers whenever you're in a stage of major transition—thinking of marriage, getting a new job, buying a home, preparing for retirement, or reentering the job market. Pay special attention to clarifying your objectives during these times.

How often you review your answers depends on your situation. Whenever I am going through a major transition, I review mine every Sunday. Use any timetable that will keep your objectives up to date so you can get the most from your time every single day.

Defining your objectives helps you pick your activities. It's only common sense to find the target before firing, yet how often is this logic overlooked? How many times have you heard someone suggest forming a committee before the committee's purpose has been determined? A committee may not be the best way to achieve the desired objective. Perhaps it's a job for one person.

Use a Yardstick

When your objectives are specific, you will stay on target. Here's a handy yardstick for designing specific, workable objectives. It includes the four key elements in the classic definition of an objective: result, standard, target date, and cost in terms of time and money. Here are two examples of how it works:

1. You want to increase the average order your customers place (result) by at least five percent (standard) no later than December 31 (target date) at a cost not to exceed $250 and 20 hours of your time (cost).

2. You want to meet three new people (result) with whom you'd be happy to spend at least a few hours each week (standard) before November 15 (target date) at a cost not to exceed $100 and ten hours of your time (cost).

If you decide on Objective 2, you'll get off track and waste time if you spend the time prior to November 15 playing bridge with old friends rather than joining a new discussion group at your church or becoming a volunteer for your favorite political candidate.

Keep Activities up to Date

Be firm about your objectives but flexible about your activities. Realize that although your objectives may not change, the best way to achieve them may.

Keep your objectives up to date by taking a periodic fresh look at your activities. Analyze them in terms of what you want them to produce. Ask yourself, "Just why am I doing this?"

A clear, up-to-date statement of your lifetime accomplishments and lifestyle serves as a beacon that can guide you in daily life. Writing a statement of your life purpose does the same. They help you focus. New opportunities can loom on the horizon, and you may decide to alter course. But without any beacon at all, there's no easy way to know if you are headed in the right direction.

The Direction of Getting Married

Ginger liked her job in an insurance company, but she didn't need to write a Wants Inventory to know she wanted to get married. So during her daily time of prayer and Bible study, she prayed fervently: "Dear God, please bring Your husband for me to me."

Yet the more she prayed for God's husband the more she was reminded of a sentence in the book of Proverbs that she had read and didn't like thinking about.

> The rich rule over the poor, and the borrower is servant
> to the lender (Proverbs 22:7).

She particularly didn't like thinking about this guidance in the Bible on the first of the month when credit card statements started piling in her basket of bills on her kitchen counter. One month, she opened them all, spread them out on her table, took a small calculator, and did something she had not done before. She totaled—not the minimum payment—but the entire amount due. She totaled it twice because she couldn't believe it was over $14,000. She had never thought much about money because she was sure she was going to get married, but this was staggering.

That night as she got ready for bed, she still prayed for God's husband for her. The next night after a long and distracted day, she sat at her table and told God that she wanted to be His servant and not a servant to credit card lenders and that she was going to do what the Bible was guiding her to do. Get out of debt.

It took a class on biblical money management. It took persistence. It took finding a roommate to share the rent. And it took saying no to herself hundreds of times whenever she walked through a store. Even with all that, it took 19 months before she could have what she calls her party to bake a credit card pie. It was an exciting party when she sat at her kitchen table with her roommate, clipped her paid-off credit cards into chunks, spread them on an aluminum pie pan, and baked them in the oven until they melted into a memorable collage.

Ginger laughs when she shares this story, and she says the man she later met and married loved the way she could bake a pie.

Aim at Wise Action

Pray for God's guidance and power. Know what you want. Set objectives. Act on what God shows you. And step into the light He is shedding on your path.

The action steps for setting helpful objectives are:

- Keep walking ahead as you pray and ask God to direct your life and your desires.
- Define what you want—Write a Wants Inventory frequently.
- Determine lifetime accomplishments and lifestyle.
- Make short-term decisions with long-range objectives in mind.
- Work backwards. Pick objectives or targets first, then activities.
- Do something every day toward achieving the objectives and lifestyle you most want.
- When God puts a new objective in your heart, pursue it and feel His joy.

Chapter 13

What Happens When You Do Central and Essential Priorities Now

Three times a day he got down on his knees and prayed,
giving thanks to his God, just as he had done before.

Daniel 6:10

What's Ahead?
- *A quick demonstration to help you do Central and Essential Priorities now.*
- *How to cut stress and save time by labeling a time pressure or opportunity as a Central Concern or Essential, a Secondary Matter, or a Marginal Matter.*
- *When 80 percent gets an "A."*

When one Bible study series starts, the over 200 women in the class know what will be part of the first class. The teacher of the study brings out the same demonstration every year to encourage the class members to do Central and Essential Priorities first. To start the demonstration, she puts two jars on the table at the front of the room, and people start to smile and laugh because they know what will happen. Then she puts near each one of them a bowl of Ping-Pong balls and a bowl of rice. To emphasize the power of doing the big important tasks first, she pours the rice into the first jar. It's over half full as she asks the group to call out the "rice" priorities they can encounter during a day. With the jar over half full of rice, she tries to pour the Ping-Pong balls into the same jar only to see them spill over the table and bounce along the floor.

Then she pours the Ping-Pong balls into the other jar, which is empty, and emphasizes what happens when you do the most important priorities first. Although the jar is full of Ping-Pong balls, it will still hold the rice. It's all a matter of doing the Central and Essential Priorities first and doing them now. This is one of those easier-said-than-done ideas. This calls for prayer, Bible study, and practical skills.

Why not just put time skills to work? Why emphasize the role of Bible study and prayer in doing the most important priorities first and now? Here's why. Time demands don't march into your life in orderly ranks, waving banners with preassigned priorities. Most often they resemble an unruly mob, crowding in at once and competing for your time and attention. Even though you know it isn't possible, they may all seem to be waving banners that say, "I'm the most important." Your prayerful perspective helps you understand the real priority.

Knowing what has the highest priority right now is the first step toward doing what really counts. The key is to develop a flexible system you can use to assign an up-to-date priority to each demand, problem, opportunity, objective, and activity.

Every time a demand in that unruly mob calls for your attention, pray and consider what priority it really should have right now. You are the only one who knows your situation well enough to give potential time investments accurate priorities. You are the only one who cares enough about your time situation to make those priorities stick. Be firm but not rigid. You can learn when to stay with something important, even under pressure. You also can learn when to change your course. If you keep your priorities open for revision, you'll be less likely to abandon them at a crisis point.

Don't cheat yourself by saying, "It's not that easy!" It isn't easy, but it is worthwhile. Learn to assign priorities accurately and stick with them. You will make decisions faster, relieve frustration, and clear up guilt.

Keep Your Time on Target

Picturing time demands in terms of a target has helped thousands of people I've worked with. Imagine a target with three circles.

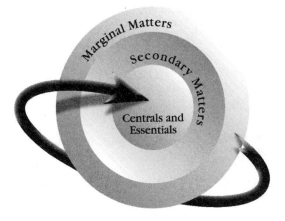

Fig. 13.1

As you can see in the diagram, the arrow is aimed straight at the center of the target, because you get the most from your time by starting with Central Concerns and Essentials.

Central Concerns and Essentials—The Best Place to Begin

Central Concerns are what you most want and value in life—your major priorities. They are important but not urgent. They relate directly to the most important contributions you make on your job and in your service to other people. They are what you discovered when you used the one hundredth birthday technique. They are your answers to the questions about your long-term accomplishments and lifestyle. They are the result of working with the special strengths and gifts God has given you.

Essentials are what you must do in the course of the day to stay alive, healthy, and able to pay the rent. They are important and *also* urgent. Many Essentials are maintenance activities. Brushing your teeth is an Essential. Paying taxes is an Essential. Meeting a deadline on your job can be an Essential. If the 7:10 is the only bus that will get you to work on time, catching it is an Essential.

Essentials call attention to themselves. However, for every real Essential there are a dozen falsely claiming this priority. There is the salesperson who insists that you buy a car today because you'll never find another one, the coworker who interrupts your concentration because he has just one more opening in the pool for the Super Bowl. These demands may be urgent, but they are not essential. The real Essentials cannot be left undone.

Secondary Matters—The Treacherous Middle Ring

Secondary Matters are demands that may be worthwhile, but they are not the best things to be doing now. This middle circle is the most misunderstood, and potentially the most dangerous. Secondary matters are worthwhile, but they won't give you an optimum return on your time investment. They don't offer the greatest rewards and satisfactions. They do not contribute the most to your lifetime accomplishments. They don't relate the most closely to your long-range lifestyle. They are not the most important part of your job. They are good, but they are not the best way to invest your time right now. It is true. The enemy of the best is the good.

Marginal Matters—The Outer Circle

Marginal Matters include the hundreds of relatively trivial demands that add little value yet steal chunks of your day. These are the small, bothersome, time-consuming little jobs that can eat up your time: dusting the knickknacks, straightening up your desk, updating all your files, cataloging the slides of Yellowstone, organizing the closets. Many people feel that effective time use begins with these trivial concerns. They believe that until they get these jobs done, they won't be able to complete the important tasks. Not so. Work expands to fill the time available. This outer circle has the least value in terms of contributing to what you most want. That's why these Marginal Matters deserve the lowest priority. You'll find that many of them don't even need to be done at all—ever. You can do your financial planning, invest in real estate, write that bestseller, and develop meaningful relationships even if your desk looks messy and your slides aren't cataloged.

Getting the True Picture

Periodically updating your answers to the questions about your lifetime accomplishments and lifestyle—spotlighting your objectives—can help you give accurate labels to time demands and opportunities. Your review may reveal that a demand that was a Central Concern six months ago now isn't.

For example, a hardworking sales representative's long-range objective is to be VP of sales. His short-term objective is to acquire management experience. He is promoted to regional sales manager, in charge of six other salespeople. His first priority used to be selling to his accounts. Now that is secondary to his new management responsibilities: planning, training, and developing the sales staff. There's nothing wrong with spending his time selling, but it's just not the best investment of his time today.

If you spend a great deal of time on worthwhile tasks, but seldom experience the joy and deep satisfaction of real accomplishment, you are probably investing too much time on Secondary and Marginal Matters. Study your daily time investments. How do they relate to your long-term accomplishments and lifestyle? How do they contribute to what you are paid to produce on the job? Turn to your most recent list of objectives in your Time Notebook. Read over your last Wants Inventory. Are your activities up to date with what you want less of, want more of, and want most? Stay in touch with how your activities contribute to your objectives and wants. It's the best way to avoid wasting time on those outer circles.

What Really Counts

If this were to be your last day on the job, is there anything you would regret not accomplishing? If this were your last day on earth, is there anything you would regret not doing? Not saying?

Central Concerns, like so many opportunities, do not yell at you. They are quiet companions. Unless you are up to date on what you want and what others want, opportunities easily pass by without a sound. You'll only sense an emptiness, a dull void symptomatic of a valuable opportunity lost. Reach out and invite opportunities into your life. Don't wait for them to shout for your attention. Knowing what you want and recognizing opportunities go hand in hand. Opportunities are resources that you can use to get what you want and help others get what they want. If you haven't bothered to keep up to date on wants, you won't recognize opportunities.

A periodic review of your Wants Inventory will also give you a handle on these Central Concerns. Your daily appointment with yourself will help you generate insights about what is central. And don't forget to ask the people you work and live with what they most want. You will be able to relate to them much more effectively.

Consider these ideas frequently, act on your insights daily, and you will live a life rich with meaning.

Stay Ahead of the Game—Aim Essentials Toward Central Concerns

There are times when Essentials must take top priority. We may not want to do them, but we must do them anyway. When this occurs, there's a way to increase the value of the time you invest. Always aim essential activities toward areas of Central Concern. For example, the subject of the report you must write today may not be a Central Concern. Learning to write clear, concise prose may be. Concentrate on this aspect of the task and increase the value of your time investment.

This technique works in your personal life too. A mother of three decided that raising children who could think for themselves was a Central Concern for her. Doing the weekly grocery shopping was an Essential. She found a way to turn this Essential toward her Central Concern. Every week she took one of the young children to the supermarket. They each learned to select items from the shelves, weigh produce, and compare prices. They gained experience in making decisions and thinking for themselves. Their mother wound up with a lot more than groceries. She turned an Essential that wasn't very interesting into a high-quality time investment that her children still talk about.

Central and Essential Priorities Come First

Knowing what is central and essential to you is the first step in assigning priorities. Now picture that target diagram again. Remember how the arrow sweeps over the first two circles and goes right for the heart? That's because doing Central and Essential priorities first is the fastest way to find more time.

Label Every Potential Time Investment

Whenever you have a potential time investment, assign it a rating in the target diagram:

1. For Central Concerns and Essentials

2. For Secondary Matters

3. For Marginal Matters

Do this for each interruption, letter, telephone call, or idea that pops into your mind. When someone asks you to do something, immediately clarify what priority the job has for them. When you ask for help, let people know what kind of priority it is for you.

Continually direct your mental energies, attention, and excitement toward the center of the target. You will feel pressures pulling you toward Marginal and Secondary Matters. Ignore them. Learn to recognize the Marginal Matters right away and skip over them. Avoid Secondary Matters as much as possible. Give first priority to that inner circle. When you must do something essential, aim it toward a Central Concern.

The 80/20 Ratio—Picking Each Job's Vital Ingredients

When you feel you're getting swamped by too many jobs that are truly central or essential, there is a technique that can help. It's called "picking the vital few ingredients," and evolves from principles formulated by Italian economist Vilfredo Pareto. Pareto's law states that 80 percent of the results come from 20 percent of the causes. The point is to work on the vital few causes and you will accomplish most of the result.

Identify the vital ingredients necessary to achieve your objective. Do these things first. You will get the most results in the least amount of time.

The first step in using this tool is defining your objective clearly. Then discover what the vital ingredients are in that accomplishment. It isn't always easy, because individual situations differ. Here are some examples that will give you a start.

Experts have analyzed hundreds of causes in the objective of eliminating the enormous number of highway fatalities. They came up with a startling fact. If we could keep drunk people from driving, we could reduce traffic fatalities by 75 percent. Just one cause has more effect than all other causes combined.

The typical clothes closet is a classic example. Here's the objective: To look good and feel good in what we wear and also to dress quickly. Think of all the causes of this result hanging in our closet. However, if you are like most people, a few favorite garments account for how we look most of the time. They are the clothes we look our best in. They are the articles of clothing we reach for day after day. They make the major contribution to our daily style and appearance.

Your closet may hold many other garments that you seldom wear. Some are suitable only for special occasions. Others were impulse buys that don't fit well or just don't go with anything else. Another might be the sweater someone special gave you that doesn't quite look right but still feels warm with sentiment. Because you seldom wear any of these, they produce a small part of your everyday look. The few favorite outfits you wear most often create that. They are the vital few causes of looking good and feeling good in what you wear.

Analyze Activities Before You Dive In

Imagine that you have just returned from a three-week vacation and picked up your mail. There's a stack two feet high. How much do you have to read right away?

First, decide what your objective is. Perhaps you only want to read the mail necessary to keep your life running smoothly for the next few days. Probably you'll have to read much less than 20 percent of the stack.

Sort through the mail looking for vital ingredients. For example, there's a letter from the tax board, and your taxes are due in three days. That letter is a vital ingredient. There's a colorful folder describing a dozen cruises to the South Seas. That's not a vital ingredient. If you have no interest, toss it. Otherwise, put it in a separate pile. There's an offer for a magazine subscription, a notice about the opening of a new boutique next week, and a brochure about a new insurance program. Anything that doesn't contribute to the result you want—a smoothly running life for the next three days—gets tossed or goes into the second pile. They aren't vital ingredients. Read the mail in your vital ingredients pile first. It's delightful how much of your second pile you can toss directly into the recycling wastebasket.

What Went Wrong?

One of the best ways to sharpen your skill in identifying the vital few causes is to analyze why some activity or project went wrong. When you don't achieve the results you want, pinpoint what was missing.

Evie complained one day that the dinner party she'd given the night before disappointed her. She'd looked forward to an evening of good conversation with friends she rarely saw, but somehow it didn't come off. She spent hours shopping, cooking, and arranging the table. The hot hors d'oeuvres kept her running to the kitchen. The main course of Saltimbocca kept her running to the kitchen with last-minute preparation and cooking. Dessert was a chocolate soufflé that required more last-minute preparation and split-second timing. During dinner, she was so busy changing plates and checking the soufflé that she hardly sat down. Throughout the whole evening she barely had time to talk to anyone.

First, she reviewed her objective: good conversation with enjoyable friends in a relaxed atmosphere. The vital ingredients for that didn't include preparing a four-course dinner or showing off her most elaborate recipes. The vital ingredients were the people and her presence with them.

For her next dinner party, she concentrated on the guest list and kept the details simple. She made a hearty beef burgundy stew and crisp green salad. Dessert was fruit and cheese. It saved time and money, and she achieved the result she wanted.

Learn how to identify the vital ingredients and take care of them first. This technique will help you achieve more and make you feel better. That's one of its greatest payoffs. You will feel the satisfaction of accomplishing the results you want.

What are the ingredients for one accomplishment that really matters in your life?

Pick an upcoming event such as a meeting, vacation, or dinner. What are the vital few things you need to do to make this worthwhile and enjoyable for you?

Where 80 Percent Gets an "A"

In most instances, 80 percent is all that's necessary. That email message or the weekly housecleaning doesn't have to be 100 percent perfect. Take care of the vital ingredients, and you'll achieve that 80 percent result in less time. Invest the time you save on a Central Concern. Complete the long-range planning you want to do for your organization. Spend some joyful hours with a special person in your life.

When you think of the Ping-Pong balls and rice mentioned at the beginning of the chapter, remember how when you do your Central and Essential Priorities first and do them now, much of the smaller things will also fit in. One woman in the Bible study class knew how easy it is to forget doing Central and Essential Priorities first, so she tucked a Ping-Pong ball reminder in her car, on her desk, and one on the windowsill above her kitchen sink. She laughed and reported that she has trained herself so well that if she starts doing a Secondary Matter, she hears in her mind the rattle of rice being poured.

Focusing on What Really Matters

Not everyone is going to tuck Ping-Pong ball reminders around, but find your ways to encourage yourself to use these powerful tools:

- Few things are worth doing perfectly. Find out what those few are and give them your time and attention.

- For the rest of your time demands, focus on the vital ingredients and do them first.

- Give every potential time investment a priority rating of 1, 2, or 3.

- Do Central Concerns and Essentials first—remember, everything that seems essential may not be.

- Aim Essentials toward Central Concerns.

- Pick the vital ingredients in each task and do them first.

Part IV

Overcoming Tools

To Gain Energy and Get Back on Track

OVERCOMING TOOLS

To Gain Energy and Get Back on Track

🐏 Get help for straying or stalling.

🐏 Shepherd your time. Protect it, guide it, and get it back on the path and moving ahead.

Chapter 14

Burnout—Preventing It and Getting Out of It

*Come to Me, all who are weary and heavy-laden,
and I will give you rest.*
Matthew 11:28 NASB

What's Ahead?

- The eight early warning signals of burnout.
- Your personal warning signals.
- How to prevent burnout—and how to get out of burnout.
- The one burnout remedy that makes the most difference.
- How to tackle tough times with three-way maintenance.

As I was sitting at my computer and writing this chapter, I asked myself what would be a quick and easy way that would make the main point memorable. An embarrassing story flashed to my mind that would perfectly illustrate this chapter's big idea: Maintain yourself so you can handle the tough times.

But I realized that I had not shared this embarrassing event with even the closest people in my life. Was I ready to share it now for the sake of making the point easy to remember? I decided...yes.

Driving down an eight-lane freeway several years ago, my heart was pounding as I frantically glanced over my shoulder and into my rearview mirror. My emergency lights were on. I was signaling for other drivers to let me move over to the slow lane of the freeway. My yellow Buick Century had begun to make terrible grinding sounds, and it was losing speed rapidly. With the cars and 18-wheelers whizzing by, I prayed that my car would not stall on that freeway through a rugged area of Oakland. I prayed that it would keep moving until I could get over to the side and down an off-ramp.

As I sat gripping the steering wheel, my mind raced with questions. What could possibly be the problem? Because I lived in a city and traveled most of the time, I had driven rental cars. This was the first car I had ever owned. When I bought it through the father of a friend five months ago, I was delighted to have such a good-looking car with only 23,000 miles on the speedometer. It had appeared to be in excellent condition. During the time I had owned it, I kept it washed, filled with premium gas, and parked in my garage. As I heard the noise from the engine, I wondered if my assistant had filled it with cheap gas.

The car was now barely limping, and the motor was making increasingly loud noises. I was still baffled about the cause of the problem as the car crawled slowly off the freeway, rolled down the off-ramp, wheezed an additional 300 yards, and stopped in the parking lot of a diner. As I removed the key, I still had not considered the possibility that this would be the last 300 yards my butter yellow Buick with the gray vinyl top would ever move under its own power.

When the tow truck arrived, the driver started interrogating me.

"Did you maintain it?"

"Yes."

"What kind of gas did you use?"

"The best."

I even ran my hand over the raised hood to show how clean I kept the car. As the tow truck driver leaned under the hood, he wanted to know one more thing.

"What kind of oil did you use?"

I hesitated and then asked, "Oil?"

That day I accepted his next words as a life lesson never to be forgotten.

He shook his head in disbelief, slammed the hood, and announced, "You have to give it the right maintenance or it won't keep running."

His words are the most important point to remember from this chapter, because this advice is true, not just for cars, but for your own body, mind, and spirit.

Whether we know it or not, we all need maintenance in these three areas or we won't be prepared for the tough times or be able to prevent the dangers of burnout.

Eight Early Warning Signals of Burnout

Of the eight early warning signals of burnout, the first is the most subtle. It is the most personal. And it is among the most costly.

1. Less productivity

If someone's work contribution is sagging, they are usually the first to notice.

Decisions are not as good. Operations are not as smooth. Problem prevention is not as consistent. In short, the person suspects that he is not adding as much value as usual.

2. Less communication

Less communication can take place at work. Picture the woman who usually has three or four things to contribute to every meeting. If this person is letting herself get into burnout, she might not offer any of her thoughts in a meeting. Instead, she might say to herself, "What's the point of saying anything? They wouldn't listen anyway."

Less communication can show up in a person's personal life. Picture the man sitting at the breakfast table with his bowl of Cheerios and banana in front of him. Instead of talking to his wife, he's reading the cereal box. He feels no interest in communicating.

Less communication can show up at social events. Picture the person who goes to a party, but instead of doing what she usually does—meeting people and talking—she goes to the kitchen and helps serve chips and dip. There's less communication involved.

Picture the person who goes home at night and says, "Oh, no," when he hears the telephone ring. One phone call can be one too many for the person letting himself slide into burnout.

We've seen that less productivity and less communication can happen either at work or at home. The third signpost pointing to burnout can show in both personal and professional life as well.

3. Less energy

Matt typically starts working right at eight o'clock. To do this, he arrives at work five or ten minutes early. He pours himself a cup of coffee, looks at his organizer and the tasks of the day, and gets a running start on the demands of work.

Now, as Matt nears burnout, there's a change. Instead of being at work at 7:50, he's eeeeeeeeeeeeeeek, squeaking in barely on time.

Less energy feeds the temptation to hit the snooze alarm. Less energy makes an ordinary task require extraordinary strength. And less energy feels as though someone has unplugged a person's toes and let all the vitality run out. As one man described it, "I feel like my gears are turning, but someone has dropped sand into them."

So we have three items that start with "less." Less productivity, less communication, and less energy.

4. Late more often

It is easy to see how this early warning signal goes with having less energy. Less energy means you move more slowly, and everything takes longer to accomplish. Being late is the natural consequence.

We've talked about the first four early warning signals—less productivity, less communication, less energy, and being late more often. These burnout signals are observable by others, both at work and at home. Now we are going to examine the last four—signals that are more personal. These are ones you would know about in yourself, but might not know about in others unless they confided in you.

5. Sleep disturbance

This warning signal shows up in two different ways. Having a problem going to sleep. That's the most typical. And wanting to sleep all the time. That's not as typical.

Trouble going to sleep often shows up like this. You lie in bed, willing yourself to fall asleep. Finally you do, but you wake up around 3:00 A.M. You toss and turn, and finally fall asleep again just before the alarm goes off. The sleep just before the alarm is the richest rest all night.

On the other side of sleep disturbance is wanting to sleep all the time. One time when I was letting myself get into burnout, I wanted to sleep all the time. I can remember seeing the beginning of a television program, but I never saw the end. I was asleep long before the conclusion of the show. Whether it is trouble going to sleep, or trouble staying awake, this signal is significant.

6. Appetite disturbance

Just like sleep disturbance, this early warning signal can show up in one of two ways. Typically, the problem is unplanned weight loss. Or it can be unplanned weight gain. During the same period of time when I couldn't keep my eyes open through the length of a TV show, I was also deep into appetite disturbance. One evening I can remember finishing dinner, but within an hour I was back in the kitchen, looking for something to eat. I wasn't hungry. Yet I was opening the refrigerator, looking into cupboards, and returning to the refrigerator. As I stood there with my hand on the door, I thought to myself, "Am I checking to see if something new has crawled into this refrigerator since the last time I looked?"

If you ever find yourself eating when you are not hungry or having no desire to eat, you know the label to put under that picture. Appetite disturbance.

7. Preoccupation with health and body

This signal is easy to see in others. When someone is showing extreme preoccupation with health and body, he may take the question seriously when you casually ask, "How are you?" He may tell you exactly how he is. Nothing is too minor to mention, because any problem is probably worse than it appears. If he has a headache, it may be a brain tumor. A stomachache may be the hint of a heart attack. He is painfully aware of every malfunction of his body. However, he may not go to a doctor because, "What do they know anyway?"

8. Decreased wants

Along with number one, burnout signal number eight is also very subtle.

Let's look at two different pictures. Suppose someone walks up to you in a seminar, hands you a lined yellow pad and a pencil, and asks you to write down everything you want to read, write, buy, build, visit, enjoy, catch up on, paint, organize, learn, listen to, attend, and teach.

When you are operating at your regular level, you could probably start writing on the first page of that pad, turn it over, keep writing on the second page, and continue through the third. That's because when you are at your usual energy level, you want to do a lot in life. That's a sign of a healthy person.

Now let's look at the second picture. Let's say the person approached with the yellow pad and pencil is burning himself out. Again, the request is to write everything he wants to do in his life.

This time the reaction is quite different. It might begin with a sigh. Two or three things are written. Another sigh. Another pause. Then the comment, "Oh, I don't want very much anymore."

Decreased wants—a decline in the number of things you want to do, a decline in the number of things that excite you, a decline in the number of things you feel you need to do.

Those are the eight early warning signals of burnout. It's important to pay attention to them as all of them are worth noting to prevent burnout before it affects your job performance, your personal life, and your health.

Whether you sense any burnout potential at the moment or not, there is value in placing the Eight Early Warning Signals of Burnout in a handy spot you look at frequently. A 3 x 5 card in your medicine chest might be just the place.

Why bother posting these eight burnout signals in advance? Because burnout is not like stepping off the edge of the Grand Canyon. Most people step into burnout gradually. During burnout, however, your thinking is not as clear as it typically is, so you may not be aware that you are stepping in a limiting direction.

Your Special Burnout Signals

We each may have three or four symptoms we have to watch on the general list, and then we may also have three or four specific individual signals we need to be aware of.

All these signals (both general and individual) of approaching burnout are worth putting on a 3 x 5 card and taping to the inside of that medicine chest.

Let me mention three examples of my individual signs to stimulate you to find your own early warning signs. One of my first early warning signals is that I start becoming suspicious of joy. If I see someone smiling, happy, and enthusiastic, my response if I'm burned out is to look at them, squint my eyes, and say to myself, "What a hypocrite" or "That happiness couldn't be real; they must be on something." The reason I know this is a burnout signal is that it's so different from my usual response. Normally I am delighted to see people who are happy; I want to be around people who are happy. I want to be around people who are upbeat. I enjoy thinking about good things and what could happen.

Here's an example from a friend's life. He confided in me that when he is burning himself out, and is in a group, he doesn't spend time with the type of person he normally does. When he is in a complaining mood, he looks for others to commiserate with. The complainers find each other so they can grumble together. When he's not burning himself out, he doesn't want to be around complaining people.

Another personal signal that I have learned to watch for is this: taking things personally.

This can happen on the job or this can happen in my private life. During a period when I was burning myself out, I rode down eight floors in an elevator with the chairman of a company that I worked with regularly. He didn't make eye contact with me or say his usual hello. As I walked away from the elevator, I was concerned. It didn't occur to me at that moment that perhaps the chairman of a multimillion-dollar company had other things on his mind than greeting me.

Another example of taking things personally occurred with my mother. My dear mother.

Even though over two million people had purchased my books and seen my films, even though my financial security was solid, even though my work was steady, my mother's greatest wish was that I receive a regular paycheck.

One evening after working on an assignment for an airline, I returned to my hotel room, sat on the bed, and picked up the phone to call my now-invalid mother. I mentioned that this assignment included my getting a flight attendant uniform, complete with my trainee name tag, and going on four flights.

I could hear the smile in my mother's voice and the hope in her words as she asked, "Well, honey, do you think if you do well it could work into a real job?"

I nearly bit the telephone cord in half. Feelings of hurt grew. Normally, I was able to reassure and talk my mother out of her unfounded worries; however, as I was letting myself near burnout, I was overly preoccupied with self.

At that moment a scene behind her fears came to my thoughts. It was a winter morning when I was small and up early. She stood by the kitchen window and pulled the curtains back to look at the heavy rain pouring into our backyard. She turned to my father as he stood with his hand on the lunch pail she had prepared for him to take to his job as a carpenter and quietly concluded, "It's pouring. There's no work today." Those times must have developed her deep desire for what represented financial stability—a regular paycheck. But as an adult, when I was burning myself out, I turned my attention inward, forgot what I knew, and took her comments personally.

My third personal warning is a short fuse. When I start becoming impatient, making small things a federal case, getting worked up about issues that won't matter tomorrow, I know it's the short-fuse problem and a warning I may be heading for trouble.

Whether you have any of these signals or not, I'm sure they triggered specific things in your mind that indicate the burnout dangers may be nearby.

Burnout will often feel like an eight-cylinder car running on only two cylinders and sometimes it will feel as though it's not running on any cylinders. It feels like pushing a stalled car.

As I drove my newly serviced car out of the auto dealership, I thought of the parallel between the car's needs and mine for preventing burnout. Over the months before taking my car in, I had not noticed its gradual decline in performance. Certainly on some of San Francisco's steep hills it had lacked pep, but the change was barely noticeable. Burnout often feels the same. The changes are often so gradual that if you're not paying attention, you may miss the signals.

Preventing Burnout and Getting Out of It

You may be asking, "Well, what do I do? How do I prevent burnout? How do I stay away from that trap?" Here are four specific burnout prevention tips.

1. For physical maintenance, exercise daily

There is no substitute for getting oxygen to your brain. Exercise gives you beta endorphins. Exercise reduces tension. Exercise gets more oxygen to your brain. It is impossible for the brain to work at its usual capacity without adequate oxygen. A person may think he's not being motivated properly, not being appreciated fully, not being listened to carefully. But without exercise, he may not be able to recognize any of the help being offered by others. His thinking is faulty.

Daily exercise is so important that if you were to do the other three burnout prevention steps without exercising, the others would not make a long-term difference.

2. For mental maintenance, learn daily

Maintenance to prepare yourself for tough times does not only mean physical maintenance; it means mental maintenance too. The best way to maintain mentally is to learn something daily. This is a familiar, but solid, piece of advice. Learn something new daily.

Learning something daily doesn't have to take extra time. For instance, think of what you could learn in a year by listening to audio programs as you drive. Turn commuting time into learning time.

And learning daily doesn't mean merely acquiring information. It means changing behavior.

A public health physician who received a medal from the U.S. Surgeon General was asked, "How can you test for senility?" Dr. Elizabeth Paeth Lasker said, "I've investigated a number of tests, and I have concluded that one question is the best quick test for senility." Here's her question: "Have you learned a good new habit during the last 12 months?"

Learning something daily doesn't mean just collecting a new bit of trivia; this means changing your regular behavior to a more positive form of behavior. The new habit does not mean learning to smoke. It means learning a new habit that helps you.

3. Solve problems without blaming

As we are looking at the four ways to prevent burnout, there is probably no argument about the first two. But this third item is often a surprise to people.

Blaming is like walking on a narrow road with a deep ditch on either side. You can fall into the ditch of blaming others or the other direction into the ditch of blaming self. Either way, you've fallen.

Blaming others does not work; blaming yourself does not work. What does work is staying in the middle of the road by solving problems without blaming.

Let's look first at why blaming others does not work. We've all had the experience of blaming someone else for a problem caused, a contract lost, a client alienated, a project mismanaged. But the results are harmful. That individual may cover up the truth, refuse to work with the team, or actually "get even."

And have you ever been around someone who blames herself? As she mentally beats herself up, productivity is lost and no one benefits. The secret is to solve problems without blaming.

4. Keep your tank full

This suggestion can prevent burnout or get you out of it once you're in it. Take care of your own needs and wants. Don't regularly wait for others to bring you flowers. Do good things for your spirit. Nurture yourself.

Many people grow up expecting others to meet their needs. "Parents who really care will give me what I want." "A spouse who really loves me will do special things for me." "A boss who really wants me to excel will motivate me." "Employees who are really excellent will go to extraordinary lengths to make my company succeed." If you're over 25, you've probably noticed the world doesn't work this way. You need to take responsibility to do good things for yourself; otherwise, you'll become whiny and resentful. Perhaps this story will give you an idea of something that will work to feed your soul.

As I walked into the building with Bobby, a division director of a technology company, she spoke to me of how much she liked having a fresh bouquet of roses in her office. Unfortunately, delivered roses seemed too expensive, and her husband didn't send flowers as often as she wanted them. Yet she had not given up enjoying the fragrance and beauty of roses in a crystal vase on her desk. Bobby related her solution to me. She took a

Saturday class on how to grow roses, bought rosebushes, and planted them on both sides of her driveway.

As I admired the current bouquet in her hands, she concluded that the effort was worth it. "It makes me feel wonderful to look at these pink, red, and cream roses and smell their fragrance during the day."

As we passed a woman working at her desk, she looked up and commented, "Well, I'm just waiting until someone brings me roses."

It's not hard to guess who would be the most enjoyable to work with. Taking care of your own needs and wants keeps your tank filled and keeps you from feeling resentful and dependent on other people.

I often hear people say:

"Yesterday was my birthday, and no one did anything."

"I've visited that customer four times, and he hasn't even offered to place an order."

"If people really cared about me, they would know I wanted to be on that task force."

Keep your own tank full. Do it without resentment. You will be more energetic. You will be more productive. And you will be more fun to be around.

Remember my yellow Buick Century? It didn't matter that I didn't know to put oil in my car. I still completely burned out the transmission. What you don't know can hurt you.

Whether you are talking about your car or your life, the driver of the tow truck is right.

"You have to give it the right maintenance or it won't keep running."

Chapter 15

Unlocking Your Energy by Getting Closure

On with it, then, and finish the job!
Be as eager to finish it as you were to plan it.
2 Corinthians 8:11 TEV

What's Ahead?

- One thing to check if you are spending time feeling tired.
- The surprising link between your energy and closure.
- Three ways people achieve closure.

Open almost any magazine or newsletter and you are likely to find a study or an article on how fatigue and a lack of energy hamper people today. Yet few of these articles and commentaries spotlight a major drain of energy—the lack of closure. Finishing a project releases energy and provides closure. Even if the results are difficult, knowing that something is done frees you to move on to the next thing with more energy.

However, the lack of closure surrounds us.

A manager in a software company regularly receives 200 emails a day, so she scans the lines for "Subject" and "From" and clicks the few messages that look the most important. The rest hang around until they are automatically deleted, depriving closure to many of her senders.

Another woman has a deep disagreement with a friend, and she stuffs the issue and avoids her friend. She never speaks the truth in love. She and her friend never understand their disagreement, much less resolve it. So she doesn't have closure, and neither does her friend.

A man has a garage stacked with hobbies that were started and not finished, furniture that could be repaired, sold, or given away, and even a car he no longer drives but still loves. It's easy to be surrounded by the lack of closure.

These two diagrams provide a quick feel for the lack and benefit of closure.

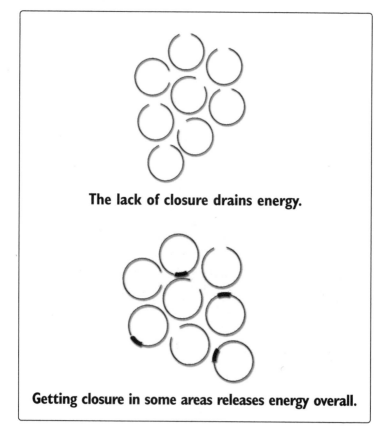

The lack of closure drains energy.

Getting closure in some areas releases energy overall.

Fig. 15.1

Getting closure is the feeling that something is completed. Off your mind. Off your list. Finished. It no longer requires active energy. When someone has closure on an issue, he or she no longer thinks of it frequently. And he or she stops talking about it constantly.

Here's a quick way to remember how lack of closure drains energy. My first computer could be lifted by the handle on the top. That little Macintosh SE was lightweight, handy, and friendly. However, it had a problem. When I opened six or seven files at the same time, the computer would get slower and slower. What that little computer was doing parallels what our human intelligence does. When a human mind has too many files open—when there is a lack of closure in too many areas—a person's thinking ability frequently starts to slow and lose effectiveness. Just as I didn't need to have seven files open at once on the little computer, neither do we need to have so many issues lacking closure.

Here's the point to remember: To free more energy, get more closure. This includes big and small issues. When you get closure, you free yourself to do something which actually increases energy: doing the right things at the right time.

Closure Through Forgiveness

> Forgive us our debts, as we also have forgiven our debtors (Matthew 6:12 NASB).

God provides us with a powerful tool for closure. It's forgiveness. When you forgive, you close the circle. You no longer spend energy on that past pain. It doesn't mean you should not take a lesson from that situation to use today, but you don't dwell on the past situation. You are free to enjoy today.

Because the benefits of getting closure are so powerful, concentrate on closure daily. Of course, there may be some areas where you won't be able to do this, so get closure where you can. You'll enjoy more energy, better concentration, and clearer thinking even when you close only some of the issues.

If you can't get closure in a big issue, aim for closure where you can and do it in a way that works for you.

Getting Closure in the Areas You Can

I've known Michael for several years, and he has always been an example of being energetic and getting the right things done at the right times. But I was still surprised one evening when I sat across a dinner table from him as he told the group what had happened to him as a teenager.

One Friday night when he was 13, Michael's father slammed the front door of their home, started the family car, and roared down the street. Michael, his mother, and his invalid sister waited uneasily and watched television as they expected Michael's father to return from buying a bottle. He had left the house like this before, but he had always come back, even though on several occasions it wasn't until a day or two later. This time they didn't hear a word. This time Michael's father didn't come back.

Michael was angry and frightened. He hated being around the house that reminded him his father was gone. So he started to hang out with older kids in the neighborhood. But a few weeks later, as he walked out of the house, he heard the front door slam shut behind him. He deliberately stopped on the front porch, turned around, looked back at the front door, and realized that he couldn't leave too. He had to help his mother and sister.

At 13 years old he started hitchhiking to the fields and working as a farm laborer after school. Some nights when he came home, he would miss his father or be angry at him, so he would sit at the kitchen table and write him a letter. He would hold the envelope with a name but no address for a moment and then slip it under his clothes in his chest of drawers.

Later, when Michael put on his cap and gown for high school graduation, he wished his father could see him and wondered what it would have been like to look into the audience and see his father smiling back. The next day Michael was still sorry his father had never gotten to know that he had graduated from high school even though his father had not. So Michael sat down at the kitchen table and wrote him another letter.

Then Michael joined the Air Force. He sent much of his pay to his mother, who took care of his now wheelchair-bound sister as she struggled with advancing multiple sclerosis.

After his honorable discharge, he enrolled in college and began a full-time accounting major while working full-time as a night auditor. The job served his purpose. It allowed him to study at a back desk when he finished his work early. By this time, he rarely missed his father except on an occasional Friday night. Michael still wished his father had gotten to know him and that he had gotten to know his father. At moments when he missed him the most, or was angry at him, he would take out a legal pad and write him a letter expressing all his feelings. Michael now kept the letters in a big envelope in a filing cabinet.

Michael went on to complete his four-year degree, his master's degree, and his CPA certification. His days of hard work were paying off as he now enjoyed a bright future at a big accounting firm. He bought a house on a hill and installed a redwood deck and a hot tub. After his sister died, he took his mother to Paris for a week, and settled down to what he thought would be a peaceful life.

Then late one night at his mother's home in Los Angeles, there was a knock on the door. After 19 years of no news, standing there was his father with big news. Michael's father had just been diagnosed with terminal liver cancer. And now he was begging Michael's mother to take him back.

I'm hoping you want to know what Michael and his mother did, but let's pause in this story for a moment just to emphasize how the human mind longs for closure and how to discover how you would benefit from more closure.

Where to Close That Circle

Many people ask, "How do you know if you need to get closure?" These questions can help you find the clues that closure is needed.

- When you look at your garage, what closure rating would you give it? Is there exercise equipment you might decide to use? A chair you don't want to tell Aunt Ethel you no longer like? A hobby someone started and then lost interest in?

- When you look in your clothes closet, do you see garments you don't like but hesitate to give away?

- Is there a difficult situation that is long past but you still talk about it?

- Do you talk about a problem repeatedly, yet choose not to do whatever you can towards resolving it? (It's like constantly stirring a pot of mud without emptying any or all of the pot.)

- Do you ever talk with person A about how person B wronged you?

- Do you ever want person A to agree with you and say, "You're right. Person B is terrible! I can't believe you were treated that way."

- When person C makes a mistake or has a problem, do you ever secretly smile?

These aren't the only clues of a lack of closure, but they are good indicators of energy wasted and opportunities lost.

Getting Closure with No Temporary Parking Places

Leaving papers or keys in temporary parking places on your desk or around your home can add to the lack of closure. A person's mind wants to remember that the bills to be paid were left on top of the newspaper that had been read. The mind also works to keep track of the keys that are in the coat pocket rather than on the hall table. And what about the doctor's appointment card that is now on the car seat? Because the mind longs for closure, these temporary parking places drain energy. That's why one of the top ideas people tell me after a speech is this: In use or in place. No temporary parking places.

Fig. 15.2

Copies of this small sign have shown up in many offices, and I'm told it's in quite a few homes. If a document or an object has an important purpose, take the time to give it a special place. Its regular parking place. Where you put it is less important than the fact that it has a specific location. It's very frustrating to search for something you've put in a temporary parking place because you hadn't decided what to do with it. I'm such a Category Two in this area that I decided that before I buy something there needs to be a regular parking place for it first.

Getting Closure with a Not-to-Do List

Peter F. Drucker recommends this on an executive level, and I recommend it on every level. It's easy to feel tired and drained when you think of everything that you could or "should" be doing. When you move something to your Not-to-Do list, you close that circle. You eliminate that slight drain of energy. In addition, when you have thought through your Not-to-Do list, it is easier to say no. It is easier to remember that you are not procrastinating on a task; you are never going to do it!

You might ask what kinds of things go on a Not-to-Do list. I have asked hundreds of people to stand up in conferences and say aloud something they are putting on a Not-to-Do list. Some of the items are funny; some are serious.

"I'm never going to clean out my garage."

"I'm never going to sort out my box of pictures."

"I'm never going to weed and mow that yard. I'm hiring a gardener."

"I'm never again sitting on the bleachers in a rainstorm at a football game. I'm getting a comfortable chair, a big-screen TV, the sports channel, and a kitchen full of chips and dip."

This list illustrates how getting closure can refer to big issues or boxes of pictures. In addition to variety in the size of the subject of closure, you'll find variety in the "how" of closure.

The How of Getting Closure

We've looked at content aspects of getting closure, but there is almost a mechanical side in how we gain it. Three main channels for getting closure are Seeing, Hearing, or Action. When you know how you prefer closure, you can achieve it more rapidly and effectively.

1. Seeing closure is effective for many people

Putting things in writing is a powerful form of closure for many people. In the story we haven't finished, Michael eased his pain and achieved his closure by writing letters to his father. Mention journaling to a group, and you can tell in a moment who the seeing-closure people are. They smile. The people who get closure in another method groan when they hear "journaling."

Here's a funny example of seeing closure. One afternoon at a conference with Buckminster Fuller, over 200 people were gathered in a lodge overlooking Lake Tahoe. We had been invited to listen to the inventor of the Geodesic Dome and hear his ideas on how to live with beauty and yet use our resources wisely.

As the weeklong conference progressed, people started asking the famed theorist more personal questions. Everyone laughed when they heard this question from one of his devoted students. This person asked why Bucky wrote books that even his most enthusiastic students could not understand.

Buckminster Fuller smiled and answered without hesitation, "I write books so I can have more room for new ideas."

Another example of seeing closure is the person who hangs up the telephone and feels an urge to write a thank-you note to the person he has just talked with on the phone.

Or consider the picture of the staff member who goes into her manager's office, talks about a decision, and hears about a path of action. But as the staff member turns to walk out the door, her manager utters the statement the staff member hates to hear, "Will you put that in writing for me?" Her manager is another example of someone who gets closure by seeing.

When one man in the audience heard this example, he groaned and said out loud, "So that's why when I talk with my wife about a problem she puts a letter on my pillow."

2. Hearing closure satisfies other people

Patricia is like many salespeople. When she closes a big sale she can hardly wait to pick up her phone, call in to the office, and hear herself say, "I got the order." Patricia and many others feel a sense of closure by talking about the issue. She is not motivated by paperwork and credit approvals. She has psychologically closed the sale when she says, "I got the order." Typically, the credit manager and the customer satisfaction people do not share her style of closure. She is usually the one they have to call four and five times to get her to finish the paperwork.

3. Action closure is the preferred way for some people

Don gets closure by slipping the file on his desk in the drawer as soon as he finishes with it. He moves papers off his desk. He snaps documents into the binder when he is finished with a discussion. At home on the weekend when he works on a project, a hammer never rests on the workbench overnight. He hangs it on the Peg-Board as soon as he finishes. He gets closure through action.

Generous Judy enjoys giving gifts that are exactly on target with what people enjoy. She looks at the electronic thank-you cards she receives, but she smiles and feels she hit the mark when she rips open the envelope to a physical thank-you note. Judy gets a sense of closure through action.

There is no one right way of achieving closure. The important thing is to know the way you get closure and then get it in the areas you can.

Michael's Closure

As you hear the rest of the story about Michael, you'll find it even easier to remember how getting closure frees energy to do the right thing at the right time.

When Michael received the telephone call from his mother that his father had come back, had cancer, and was begging his mother to take him in, Michael was shocked. Then he was enraged. The entire week after his mother first called him with the news, Michael refused to return any of the phone calls from his father.

The next Friday night as Michael sat in his hot tub with three friends, feeling the warmth of the water and talking about the situation with them, he realized what the real issue was. He was not responsible for his father's drinking. He was not responsible for his father abandoning his mother and sister and him. He was not responsible for getting even. He was not responsible for teaching his father a lesson. On the other side, he was responsible for doing the right thing. And he was responsible for doing it no matter what his father had done.

Energized with his new insight, Michael stepped out of the hot tub, reached for the telephone, and called for a flight reservation for the next day. As he boarded the plane to see his father, he said that he didn't know what he was going to do, but his commitment was to do the right thing no matter what his father had done.

That flight turned into one of many to Los Angeles to visit his father. Michael took time off work and helped take his father to his chemotherapy treatments. He brought him home from the hospital. He filled out forms for the insurance. Michael spent hours with his father and for his father.

Michael summarized what happened during those last six months: "I got to know him first as son to father, then as man to man. I finally knew who he was. And my father finally knew who I was—when he died in my arms."

Reduce Your Mental Overload

Even though I have known this story for some time, it still touches me and reminds me to put into practice the principle of getting energy by getting closure in the areas and the ways that you can. Then use that energy to do the right things at the right times.

- Closure pays. It hands you more energy, better concentration, and clearer thinking. Remember that small Macintosh SE computer that slowed to a crawl when it had six or seven files open? Even though your mind is a million times more profound, you work better when you don't have many issues "open" at the same time.

- Adopt the habit of getting closure in the areas you can.

- Get closure in the ways that work for you whether it is through seeing, hearing, or action.

Dedicate the energy you unlock to doing the right things at the right times even if you run into procrastination.

Chapter 16

Shepherding Your Time—
For Stalling or Straying

The LORD is my shepherd.
Psalm 23:1

What's Ahead?

• Why shepherding your time helps procrastination more than scolding yourself.

• How a procrastination profile helps you prevent problems.

• Cutting procrastination by understanding how people are motivated by what they are missing.

For most people, some percentage of their time pressures stem from stalling, straying, and procrastinating. Some say that the only thing you should do is pray more. Procrastination certainly is a time to pray more. If I am procrastinating, I look for a place to be alone, and then read this quote from the Bible word by word to God in prayer:

> Live by the Spirit, and you will not gratify the desires of the sinful nature. For the sinful nature desires what is contrary to the Spirit, and the Spirit what is contrary to the sinful nature. They are in conflict with each other, so that you do not do what you want (Galatians 5:16,17).

Then I add: "Dear God, I'm not doing the things that will please You and that I want to do. Please help me walk in the power of Your Spirit. Thank You for Your promise that when I do this, I will not carry out the desire of my human nature."

Procrastination is also a time to use the understanding and tools that will help you move in the direction that will please God. And it's also a time to look at your time in a new way—the way a shepherd looks at his sheep. We have Jesus, our Good Shepherd, as our guide, and we become an undershepherd as we imitate Him in caring for a precious resource God has given us—our time.

Shepherding Your Time

This means thinking about your time in a new way. Rather than trying to manage it, start shepherding it. Know it. Take care of it. Protect it. Guide it. The metaphor of shepherding your time is a seminar in a sentence. When I ask people to think of themselves as a shepherd for their time, they automatically know things to do. Just think what you would do if you were a shepherd taking care of sheep.

You would certainly know where your sheep are and where they have been. Yet few people have a good idea of where their time goes. When they think of shepherding their time, they keep better track of it.

When you shepherd your time, you treat it with more kindness. You protect your time. You make sure your flock has the right nourishment. You think ahead so that you don't let your sheep run out of food or walk off a cliff. You anticipate problems, and you guide those sheep around them. If a sheep falls into a ravine, you don't stand on the edge of the ravine and yell, "You should have..." You pull it out, take care of it, and get it moving in the right direction.

Understanding Procrastination Patterns

For some of us, procrastination is a means of getting negative stimulation and excitement. (Remember those last-minute rushes to meet a deadline?) For others, procrastination is a response to those messages we learned from our parents. People who adopt defiant behavior patterns as children may wind up procrastinating as adults. It's one more way to "show 'em."

In this chapter, we're not going to look at the why as much as the how of procrastination. When you recognize a pattern, you have a better opportunity to know what will help prevent procrastination. The first step is learning how to chart your own "Procrastination Profile."

Rate Your Quota

To begin plotting your Procrastination Profile, think about your Stimulation and Excitement Quota. How much stimulation and excitement do you need—a lot, a little, something in between? Do you find yourself in a breathless last-minute rush a couple of times a week? Do you find yourself dashing to make the bus every morning? Do you often involve others in a last-minute rush to help you meet a deadline? Do you feel somewhat bored when things are going too smoothly? Ask the people you work or live with for their opinions of your Stimulation and Excitement Quota. They know more than you might suspect.

Now rate your quota on this subjective scale:

Your Stimulation and Excitement Quota

Low	Medium	High

Out in the Open or Behind Closed Doors

Next, consider how you handle procrastination in terms of your relationships with other people. Do you internalize it, keeping it confined to a dialogue between you and your nagging conscience? Or do you grab hold of anyone who will listen and talk about what you have to do, the difficulty you have meeting the deadline, or how you just can't get down to doing what you feel you should be doing?

Do you go even further and involve others in your behavior—like the star who gets everyone into the act to help her make the curtain for each performance?

Know What You're Avoiding

In addition to providing stimulation, procrastination also is a way of avoiding feelings—most often, feelings of success, enjoyment, or closeness. Many people procrastinate to avoid the feeling they would have if they finished a task—not just to avoid the task itself.

For example, Richard was a competent executive who handled his job responsibilities for years by working overtime nights and weekends. The company realized he could handle a higher-paying position if they freed him from some of the work, so they hired an assistant for him. Richard said he felt relieved and looked forward to the promotion and the time he could now spend with his family. But he never seemed to have time to train his new assistant to take over his old workload. Achieving greater success in his career generated mixed emotions. Getting closer to his family was something he desired but didn't quite know how to handle. He kept these unfamiliar feelings of success and closeness at bay by procrastinating.

Some people avoid closeness by procrastinating on thank-you notes. They neglect to write the note and then hope they don't encounter the person. They cut down opportunities for contact and closeness by procrastinating.

If you procrastinate, what is it about? Specifically, what would you be doing or feeling if you went ahead and did what you're avoiding? Remind yourself that it's fine to feel closeness, enjoyment, and success. You can know what you are feeling, and you can feel what you are feeling. Many people find it calming to name a feeling. Remind yourself that feeling something and putting it into action are different.

The When of Procrastination

Another factor in procrastination is when. Do you procrastinate most often at the beginning of a project? Do you have trouble getting started? Or do you find your resolve crumbling and your energies evaporating at the end, when you need that last big push to finish the job? If you analyze when you procrastinate, you can work around that critical point by reinforcing yourself when you need it most.

Early Warning Signals Tip You Off

Next, give some thought to how you procrastinate. When you have mixed emotions about a project, do you suddenly become inappropriately fatigued? Do you get so hungry that you have to run out for a double-decker banana split before you can get down to work? Other typical delaying tactics include cleaning your nails, straightening up your desk, catching up on non-essential paperwork, or scheduling a conference with coworkers to make sure everyone is "up to date." One software engineer told me that when he needed to study for a big exam was when he actually spent extra hours on Bible study. How much better than the more common habit of putting the studying off by ordering a pizza.

Recognize the early warning signals that will tip you off to your own procrastination ploys. Take helpful action before you let them take over. (You will learn how in the next chapter.)

Chart Your Profile—Spotlight "Prevention Points"

Shade in the marked areas on the Procrastination Profile diagram. Fill in the boxes that spell out most accurately your assessment of the various aspects of your own procrastination pattern. When you've finished, you'll have your own personal profile.

This will help you spot when and why you procrastinate and give yourself special help at those points. It's the first step in learning how to put procrastination in its place.

Your Procrastination Profile

Your Stimulation and Excitement Quota:	Very low	Fairly low	Average	High	Very high
How You Handle Procrastination:	Internally		By talking to others		By involving others
When You Procrastinate in a Project:	Very low		In the middle		Toward the end

What You Procrastinate About

Projects that could mean feeling greater success and importance:	Not very often	Frequently	Always
Things that might result in your feeling closer to others:	Not very often	Frequently	Always
Things that mean you're feeling forbidden feelings, such as joy, ease, confidence, or peace:	Not very often	Frequently	Always

Fig. 16.1

Procrastination Prevention

Now that you've charted your personal Procrastination Profile, you have a better handle on the specifics of procrastination. The next step is to build on this knowledge and develop an effective program of procrastination prevention. The three keys are:

1. Maintain your S&EQ at the level best for you.

2. Discover what motivates you.

3. Direct your energy. Make your Central Concerns and Essentials appealing and exciting to you.

Keeping Your Gauge on Full

Visualize your S&EQ as a gas gauge on an automobile dashboard. When the gauge is on full, you eliminate the unnecessary stress of worrying about a fill-up. If you ever had the experience of driving with an almost-empty gas tank late at night, you'll know this kind of stress. You will turn into any station, even if it doesn't sell the brand of gas you really want.

The same thing happens in terms of time. If your gauge is low, you will seek any stimulation, even negative. When your supply is full, you can be selective and choose what's best for you.

After charting her Procrastination Profile, Brenda realized she needed a high level of stimulation. She worked out a method of keeping her gauge on full by planning her weekends a month in advance. She made sure she had enough activities scheduled to give her the stimulation she needed. She chose a range of activities that included a new improvement project at work, get-togethers with friends, tickets for a football game, training for a marathon, redecorating her apartment, and organizing a church picnic.

Connie was an auditor who traveled constantly. She got around her old stress-inducing need to dash to the airport at the last minute by building an extra half hour into her regular departure routine. She spent that time in the airport lounge with her laptop plugged into email. The excitement of keeping up to date, responding to business demands, or sending newsy emails to her grown son and daughter more than substituted for the adrenaline charge she used to get by racing breathlessly to the boarding gate.

When you're facing a time project, check your gauge. Do you have a full supply of stimulation and excitement? If it's only half full, or seriously low, take steps in advance to keep it topped off.

Switching from Negative to Positive

One of the most challenging aspects of procrastination prevention is the substitution of positive stimulation and excitement for negative. A simple subtraction of negative excitement isn't usually enough. You will need to add an equal amount of positive stimulation.

Denise knew her responsibilities as a full-time homemaker were important, but she also discovered that few people noticed her work at home, and her small children never gave her the applause her coworkers did when she was a buyer at a clothing store.

She found herself stalling, straying, and procrastinating. In the evening, when her husband returned from his job and commute, she would frequently just be starting to think about what to prepare for dinner. When they were getting ready to go to church, she would be scrambling to find socks that matched and clothes that still fit her fast-growing six-month-old and three-year-old. When the children were quiet in the afternoon, and she could tackle some of her housework, she found herself sitting on the couch reading a romance novel. Denise knew what to do. She just didn't do it. She was stalling and straying.

Finally one evening after she and her husband had an argument over a cluttered kitchen and a late dinner, she stood at the sink and told herself, "This is too much." Then she pushed aside the papers and dishes on the dining table, sat, prayed, and planned. She realized that she longed for much more positive stimulation than her children could give and than her husband would give.

So she called a friend she had met in her Bible study group for mothers of preschoolers. They agreed to be part of an "applause club." When either had done something—even though it might seem small to others—she could call, explain, and get some verbal applause. Denise explained, "No one else would applaud me for getting up, getting dressed, and cleaning the kitchen before 9 A.M."

By filling the void created by the absence of negative excitement, Denise was able to change to positive stimulation and cut the procrastination. Furthermore, she found that the gauge on her S&EQ consistently stayed at a higher level than she'd ever before experienced. And she avoided the old up and down mood swings.

You're in the Driver's Seat

The dictionary defines "motivation" as inducement, incentive—something that prompts a person to act in a certain way. Many people believe they have little or no control over motivation. They have absorbed the myth that it comes from something or someone outside themselves—their boss, their job, their friends, or their family. They wait futilely for someone else to motivate them.

In reality, we all motivate ourselves. We may not do it in the right direction, or with the necessary intensity, but each of us is at the steering wheel of our own motivations. When you accept that fact, you are ready to learn how to motivate yourself even more effectively. During my years of time coaching, I developed an exciting new psychological approach that will help you discover and use your own best motivators quickly and easily in every area of your life.

Satisfied Needs Are Not Motivators

Abraham Maslow, one of the world's leading thinkers in motivation, revealed a principle that forms the basis of this practical approach. Maslow pointed out that satisfied needs are not motivators. To understand how true this is, recall your last raise and promotion. Do you remember how you went after that objective—how motivated you were? When the day finally came, you were excited. But how excited were you three or four months later? How did that now-satisfied need figure into your personal motivation a year later?

Direct the Power of Early Unsatisfied Needs

Over the years, I've discovered that Maslow's idea can be utilized to help develop a successful, ongoing procrastination-prevention program. Clarify your early (and consequently very important) unsatisfied needs, and focus on how the motivations that stem from these needs crop up in your time use today.

These motivations are always in operation. We can't shut them off, but we can redirect them if they're not being directed in the best ways. This energy is like a strong, fresh spring of water, bubbling up from deep in the earth and flowing outward at random. You can't turn off the spring, but you are free to guide its flow wherever it will serve you best.

A New Approach to Motivation

Using Maslow's concept as a foundation, here are the steps I've developed to help you discover and direct your own motivations.

1. Accept the fact that satisfied needs are not motivators.

2. Identify your early unsatisfied needs. What did you want as a child that you didn't get enough of?

3. How do these early unsatisfied needs show up in your life today?

4. Motivate yourself to do what you want to do now by attaching an early unsatisfied need to a current time demand, then ride your momentum to greater success.

How Some People Make It Work

Norman was a sales representative who struggled constantly with mounds of paperwork. When he recalled a childhood desire that had not been completely fulfilled, he remembered that he'd always been fascinated by anything on wheels—from model cars to bicycles, cars, motorcycles, and trucks. When I saw him later, he told me, "You won't believe this, but I've kept up to date on my paperwork by sitting in my new sports utility vehicle and plowing through the back orders and products changes."

Charlene's get-it-done style had earned her a company promotion to an executive position where she rated the coveted all-walnut desk, floor-to-ceiling plant, and office conference table. She realized that while she was getting started she would have to work at home several evenings a week. She carried her briefcase and laptop home faithfully, but often they sat in the hallway and went back to the office the next day without being opened.

Then, Charlene decided that her home office—the spare bed-room—was too small. She began checking the cost of remod-eling and installing sliding glass doors and a patio to create a sense of space. Then as she picked up her briefcase and looked into their living room, she remembered that one of the experi-ences she missed most as a child was "going into the living room." The living room was off-limits for the children in her family except for special occasions. As soon as Charlene under-stood her early unsatisfied need, she stopped getting bids from contractors, ordered a desk for her living room, and got down to highly motivated and productive work.

How to Make It Work for You

1. Imagine that you are five years old. You may get a better feel for what you were like then if you recall your nickname and what you looked like. If you don't remember that period of time clearly at first, make up some memories. Your mind is so creative that what you "make up" works beautifully. (The "make up" answer helps you around a temporary memory block.) Now, go ahead and jot down five things that you wanted more of when you were five. This doesn't mean that you didn't get these things at all—simply that you wanted more than you received. Give yourself five or six minutes to be creative.

2. How do these early unsatisfied needs crop up in your life today? I guarantee that they always show up, usually in sur-prising ways. Believe it or not, a comptroller of a company remembered his childhood desire to uncork his piggy bank and play with the coins. The owner of a $40,000 luxury car with all the accessories always wanted the biggest red wagon in the neighborhood.

3. Now, how can you direct these early unsatisfied needs to help you do what you need to do right now? A writer who always loved the Sunday afternoon drives his family took when he was a child found that the fastest way to work through peri-odic writing blocks was to sit and write in his car while it was parked in the driveway. A woman who adored playing dress-up

as a little girl got around her tendency to procrastinate on returning unsatisfactory merchandise by dressing up in her most fashionable outfit.

What are some of the important tasks that you have been procrastinating about? How can you use your unsatisfied early needs to accomplish them quickly? You can prevent procrastination by making your Central Concerns and Essentials attractive and exciting to you.

Like anything new, this may seem awkward at first, but give it a trial run. You'll be amazed at how powerful this type of motivation can become and how effective it can be as a means of getting yourself fully motivated and moving on to what really counts.

Double the Benefit

Janet realized that her unsatisfied early childhood need was acceptance and appreciation from her hard-working and busy mother. She had to work two jobs to support the family when Janet's father was killed in an automobile accident. As an adult, Janet understood the situation but still felt the need. As she was thinking about this one evening as she was getting ready to go to bed, she realized that she had not spent any time reading the Bible and praying, and she missed that too.

The next morning, when she sat up in bed, she realized her solution. Volunteer to help the teacher of the women's weekly Bible study class at her church. Janet knew her skills as an administrative assistant would be a welcomed addition, and she remembered how warmly her teacher had hugged her for her new commitment to study the Bible each day.

The Three R's

Your prevention program will be an ongoing success when you remember that it depends on repetition, reinforcement, and reward.

Repetition is part of the learning process; we all need to repeat new techniques over and over until they are comfortable.

Finishing fully may be a technique you have to repeat 15 times before the skill feels natural. The learning process will be easier and more successful when you build in reinforcements.

Make sure that you promote the most desirable behavior by reinforcing productive, not negative, behavior. If you procrastinate on a task, you actually make the problem worse and increase the likelihood that it will happen again. Scolding yourself by saying, "I shouldn't have done that," or "I messed up again," is reinforcement for negative behavior. Experiment with reinforcing yourself with: "I always have choices. There's always something I can do. I turn problems into opportunities." You can reinforce productive behavior by asking yourself, "What's the best thing to do right now?" This is a very powerful truth to reinforce.

Positive reinforcements are the little things you do to encourage yourself as you tackle difficult demands on your time and energy. What will lift your spirits when you're facing long hours of hard work on the job? If you are a skier, log on to the Internet and get a ski report. Take a walk to the supply room and do five minutes of clandestine calisthenics. If the specter of writing the quarterly report is haunting you, do the draft on your favorite color of paper. If you're going to spend the weekend painting your kitchen, have your favorite music and snacks on hand. Things that may seem small to someone else may give you a big lift.

You are the only one who knows what will give you added momentum. And only you can pinpoint the best time to use them. Some people get more done when they add a reinforcement as they go along. Others work better when they reward themselves at the completion of one part of the job.

Rewards are the prizes you claim when you complete your tasks. They can range from time out to enjoy a cup of coffee after reviewing the first ten pages of a dull report to a weekend in the country when you complete your taxes. Or it might be to tell an interested colleague about a project you just finished. (However, don't pick someone who might be jealous or critical.)

My wonderful husband, who is also an author, said he was spending too much time at his computer playing games, so now he rewards himself at the end of a chapter with an absorbing round of Tetris.

Many people find that reinforcements are all they need to keep moving. Others focus on the reward they'll gain upon completion of each task, and that spurs them to continued action. Discover what works best for you. It may be a combination of both.

Learn to build a lift into anything you may be putting off or avoiding. It takes a little thought and practice, but it can help you finish even the most unpleasant task in less time. Remember, though, to pick reinforcements or rewards that keep you moving in the right direction. Going to a movie when you are in a funk may make you laugh, but it may not help you accomplish what needs to be done. Your reinforcements should be directed toward your objectives; they shouldn't pull you off the track. Many things may lift your spirits, but for now concentrate on those that move you where you want to go.

Don't Kid Yourself—Prevention Pays

Sometimes in adult life we find ourselves plagued by a nagging voice left over from childhood that says, "You shouldn't need that extra help to do what you are supposed to do." The message may have been appropriate at an earlier time, but consider the problem from today's vantage point. If you had an employee who needed a periodic boost to sustain peak performance level, wouldn't you supply it if you could? It's all right to give yourself the same amount of encouragement you'd give an employee. You're not coddling yourself when you recognize what you need and find ways to meet those needs effectively. If it works for you, do it.

Physicians know that preventive medicine is the best way to keep their patients out of hospitals. In the same way, procrastination prevention can keep you feeling good and getting the right things done. That's why it's well worth your time to understand your motivations and put them to work for you today.

You can conquer procrastination when you work with these key ideas:

- Develop positive sources of stimulation and excitement that will maintain your quota at the level that's consistently best for you.
- Substitute positive stimulation for negative.
- Identify your early unsatisfied needs and put them to work as motivators today.
- Prevent procrastination. Make Central Concerns and Essentials attractive and appealing to you.
- Use the Three R's—repetition, reinforcement, and reward—to keep yourself moving in the direction you want.

Chapter 17

Emergency Care for a Bad Case of Procrastination

Be strong and courageous! Do not tremble or be dismayed,
for the LORD your God is with you wherever you go.
Joshua 1:9 NASB

What's Ahead
- Four quick steps to put yourself back on track.
- When Reinforcements and Rewards can help.
- When it's time to pull out the tool of Do It Anyway.

At one time or another, we can all lock ourselves into a seemingly hopeless time jam. When you're feeling paralyzed by time demands, it's too late for procrastination prevention. You need fast emergency care that will get you moving again, and that's what the Four-Step Treatment Plan is. It only takes about 15 minutes, and it has a long and very successful track record.

1. Clear your mind
How do you clear your mind, especially when you're feeling down and a hundred problems and upsets are racing around in

your head? Start by asking God for guidance, healing, and power. If you can find a private place to pray, get down on your knees to help your concentration. Otherwise, pray wherever you are.

Continue clearing your mind by writing a factor sheet. Jot down everything that comes to you—feelings and thoughts. Do it privately so you won't feel intimidated by anyone seeing what you've written. And if you don't like making lists, don't list them—just write your thoughts randomly anywhere you choose. Writing on sticky notes works too. Use any tactic or implement that appeals to you.

One hard-pressed manager adds his own special style to this quick-fix formula when he feels immobilized. He keeps a box full of colored marking pens and a small sketch pad in a desk drawer. When he gets himself in a funk, he tells his assistant he'll be unavailable for 15 minutes, whips out his pad and pens, and puts all his thoughts on paper in a rainbow of colors.

An attorney I know pulls out a manila folder and writes everything down with an extra soft-lead pencil she saves just for that purpose. A ballpoint pen and a few pages in your Time Notebook will work just as well. So will writing your factors on sticky notes. The important thing is to use whatever works for you and to write everything down. You might find yourself noting some thoughts and feelings like these:

- I feel rotten.

- There's just too much to do.

- I'll never get caught up.

- I hate having to tell my manager that I missed the deadline.

- The laundry is piling up again.

- I just ate four chocolate chip cookies.

- I'm overweight, and I don't get enough exercise.

- I'm mad at Chris for not calling me.

Be specific. Mention names, places, feelings. Who did it? Who didn't do it? What's not getting done? Within five minutes you will have a comprehensive factor sheet that includes most of the thoughts and feelings relating to your case of procrastination. Instead of a nebulous whirl of negative thoughts, you will have concrete items that can be resolved. You will find your mind cleared and ready for the next step.

2. Update your wants

What do you want today—right now? This step will help you sort things out so you can get a handle on Central Concerns and Essentials, not merely urgent ones.

If you are angry that Chris didn't telephone, you might want to talk to him right now, to be reassured that you still respect each other and can work out any differences.

If you hate to tell your manager that you missed the deadline on that important project, you might want to pull the project together now in spite of the setback.

If you just feel rotten, what you probably want right now is to feel great—healthy, full of energy, optimistic, and in charge.

But how do you get yourself moving when you still feel barely able to hold the pen in your hand? Take the next step.

3. Add your reinforcements and rewards

My favorite reinforcements for this step are on a sheet in my organizer that shows these quotes from the Bible pasted on a shield:

> Take up the shield of faith (Ephesians 6:16).
>
> All things are possible with God (Mark 10:27).
>
> Is anything too hard for the LORD? (Genesis 18:14).
>
> Jesus replied, "What is impossible with men is possible with God" (Luke 18:27).
>
> Now faith is being sure of what we hope for and certain of what we do not see (Hebrews 11:1).

Earlier, you learned how reinforcements and rewards can lift your spirits. Perhaps calling a friend who always gives you a laugh is a good reinforcement for you. Or you may enjoy taking your shoes off and stretching, taking a trip to the coffee machine, or walking over to look at the view from a window.

Keep a list of especially appealing rewards that can renew your energy on hand, so you won't have to stop and think about it when you need emergency care. Select whatever works best and use it quickly.

Reinforcements and rewards aren't always absolutely necessary, but they can often improve results. If an idea appeals to you, use it. On the other hand, if the thought that pops into your mind is, "That won't work for me," then skip this step and go directly to step 4. The same strategies won't work for everyone. Remember—the important thing is to feel better and mobilize yourself for action. If reinforcements and rewards won't help you in a situation like this, then do it "cold turkey."

4. Do it anyway—The "cold turkey" technique

To give yourself more perspective, compare your factor sheet with the updated wants list you wrote in step 2. Then choose items that are most essential to you right now. These will be the ones that almost jump off the page and say, "Do me now!"—like a report that your manager needs in two hours.

You may not have recognized the importance of these essential items when your head was filled with so many confusing thoughts. By putting them down on paper, it is easier to arrange them in order of priority.

Circle the "do me now" items. Shift them around a bit. Are any volcanoes erupting? Is the earth starting to tremble around a few? Is a previously quiet one starting to send out threatening bursts of steam? Which problems can wait until you're back on your feet?

Select three or four circled items that are most important. Write them down on a clean page in order of their importance. This doesn't mean that the others aren't important, but experience has proven that more than three or four can be discouraging at this moment. A longer list may tempt you to say, "It just won't work for me," or "This is too hard." When you need quick emergency care, it's better to take action on three important things than to arrange 25 in perfect priority order and then not do any of them.

These three or four items make up your action sheet. To help you concentrate and give you hope, put your action items on one page with nothing else. If you want to add an appropriately sized reward, that's fine. Keep in mind that the purpose is not to make a list, but to give you a fresh taste of the pleasure of accomplishing something that is important.

Begin at the top of your action sheet and just do it! Use reinforcements and rewards if they help; ignore that step if it doesn't add any energy or give you a boost. The important thing is to get going now! Your action steps break the logjam and give you energy. Finish crossing off the items on your action sheet one at a time. When you finish your streamlined action sheet, go back and pick three more. Do them and enjoy the energy.

A Ready Remedy for Fast Relief

The Four-Step Treatment Plan isn't something to use once and throw away. Use it any time you find yourself in a tight situation and feel unable to move forward. Inaction and passivity make a bad case of procrastination worse. Taking action on something that really counts is the fastest way to eliminate depressed feelings. This is emergency care, and it can help you out of a tight spot again and again. Put the four steps on your calendar, or on a card that you can slip into your wallet, so you'll have them at hand whenever you need emergency help.

1. Clear Your Mind

2. Update Your Wants

3. Add Your Reinforcements and Rewards

4. Do It Anyway

The Four-Step Treatment Plan is a fast remedy for getting back on your feet and moving forward in good style.

Chapter 18

The Workaholic Quiz

Take My yoke upon you and learn from Me,
for I am gentle and humble in heart,
and you will find rest for your souls.
Matthew 11:29 NASB

What's Ahead
- Ten quick questions to give you perspective and balance.
- When the answer may not be doing more.
- When work identity becomes tangled with self-identify.

The label "workaholic" is tossed around rather carelessly today, and the definition of "workaholic" is certainly not exact. I've worked with and studied hundreds of people who put in many hours every week, but they are not workaholics. They are highly productive and derive a great deal of satisfaction from their jobs. They are able to measure their work time in terms of steady movement toward accomplishing objectives that are important to them. Most significant of all, they quickly relax and forget their work completely when they want to. They have also developed the ability to pick up and get going again rapidly. Like a light switch, they are "on" or "off" fully, with little transition time in between. They practice Time In and Time Out.

Only You Can Decide

Knowing how many hours you work a week is important, but that alone will not tell you if you are a workaholic. Know truthfully why you are working. Are you working to avoid something? Pray about your balance of work and recreation. Ask for God to renew your thinking, and ask for His guidance. Television, movies, magazines, and even your friends should not be the plumb line for your assessment.

> Be transformed by the renewing of your mind (Romans 12:2).

The ten questions below can help you decide if your work ethic is in a healthy balance with your total time investment. Because so many people receive unhealthy, negative stimulation and recognition from the number of hours they work, go through this list alone. Don't discuss it with your spouse or coworkers right now. Consider each question and be honest with yourself.

Ten Key Questions

Yes   No

_____ _____ 1. Do you have a difficult time sitting still and doing nothing?

_____ _____ 2. Do you take work along with you to social or pleasurable events?

_____ _____ 3. Do you find it difficult to relax without the use of alcohol or some other substance?

_____ _____ 4. Do you frequently think about work during times of relaxation or pleasure?

_____ _____ 5. Do you sometimes enjoy having others know that you work long hours?

_____ _____ 6. Do you have trouble really letting go and allowing yourself to have fun?

_____ _____   7. When you take a day off or go on vacation, do you take a cell phone and pager so people can keep in contact with you, and if someone from work contacts you, do you feel a certain sense of pleasure and importance?

_____ _____   8. When you actually add up the number of hours a week you worked during the last four weeks, do you wish you could cut down that number?

_____ _____   9. Have you gone three or more years without taking at least a two-week vacation without work?

_____ _____ 10. Are your time investments out of balance when you consider them in terms of work, play, and love?

Although there are no absolute answers, consider making some changes if you marked four or more "Yes's."

Only you can define the role that work has in your life. Take some time to think it through. Recognizing that you have a workaholic problem isn't easy to face, but it is always better to know the facts than to coast along blindly, merely hoping that things will work themselves out.

If you are concerned about the amount of time you work, imagine what you would be doing if you didn't work at all. If you had an independent income, what would you be doing with your time? Would you enjoy whatever activity you chose, and would you know how to do it? If you grew up with a group of people who worked constantly, you may not know how to relax and have fun. Now ask yourself if you feel that you deserve your imaginary choice.

A parent may become immersed in long hours on the job to avoid facing his or her teenager's drug problem. A spouse in a troubled marriage may flee from frank discussions of the problem by taking on an inhuman workload. An individual may hide from the reality of a barren personal life by burying fears and feelings under tons of extra work. A successful executive may increase her standards of job performance to avoid the realization that she already has far exceeded her parents' expectations for her. She may be reacting to a childhood fear that if she is more successful than her parents, they won't love her.

Are Long Hours the Price of Success?

Many of the most effective and highly paid top executives I know do not work more than 40 to 50 hours a week. The 60- or 80-hour workweek does not always come with the territory of success. Yet many people use success to justify spending most of their evenings in work or in job-related entertaining. Some subtle assumptions prop up this behavior. Sometimes it is a feeling that you have to pay for your success by sacrificing some part of your personal life. This is another variation of an inability to enjoy success fully.

Another stimulus for some people who work long hours is the naked fact that their work may be more interesting than anything or anyone else in their lives. They enjoy what happens at work more than what happens at home. If that's your situation, it's healthier to face it squarely because you can always deal with life and your time more effectively when you honestly understand your motivations.

The fear of enjoyment runs so deep in many people that they compulsively occupy themselves with work and more work to prevent any rays of enjoyment from streaming into their lives. Even though this fear of feeling good isn't rational, it's very common.

Another aspect of the fear of enjoyment is the old myth that if you hold yourself back from enjoyment, you can somehow help someone else. You don't need to fear pleasure or enjoyment because it might diminish the opportunity for others to enjoy themselves. These ideas are not accurate. Replace them with more productive strategies. God invented joy. He has plenty to give.

Savoring Success

If you keep working and working because each target you achieve has an empty ring once you reach it, you may need to enjoy more fully the successes that God has given you. Thank God specifically for them. Thank Him for the abilities He has given you to use in accomplishing them. And thank Him for the opportunities He has given you. Allow yourself the full range of feelings and joy when you accomplish something. This helps pull you off that tiring workaholic treadmill of "never enough."

The Self-Employed Workaholic

Not all workaholics are in paid employment. Owners of small businesses and full-time homemakers have tough challenges knowing how much is enough. There's always something else to be done and no boss to say, "That's enough. Go home." That's why it's so important to use the techniques we've discussed for setting objectives, doing Central Concerns and Essentials now, finishing fully, and knowing what things count the most. They can help the full-time homemaker or small-business owner escape the clutches of the workaholic syndrome. They also open doors to personal freedom and quality time that are vital, especially for those carrying the heavy responsibilities of full-time homemaking.

Do the Books Balance?

If you suspect that you are a workaholic, make sure that you aren't using work as a shield to avoid something. Then, prayerfully think through and set up a healthy mixture of time invested in work, play, and love. No one else can define exactly what the right balance is for you.

Focus and balance will not automatically drift into your life, but you can develop them by managing your time thoughtfully and consistently every day. Don't fall into the common trap of wanting your employees to love you and your family to work for you. Take action to move you closer to the focus and balance that is right for you.

Justice Oliver Wendell Holmes, a hard worker and out-standing achiever, indicated the importance of constant creativity in managing your life when he said, "Life is painting a picture, not doing a sum." You deserve free time and quality relationships and you need them. A healthy amount of time for play lifts your energy. Have you ever noticed how much energy you have when you are in love? You will do better in the long run with a healthy balance.

Doing and Being—A Vital Distinction

Our capacity for accomplishments, recreation, and relationships grows from a strong sense of our personal value, our being. No amount of work and no accomplishment can confirm or challenge the value of our being, because being does not depend on doing. Doing can lead to satisfaction and the sense of accomplishment, but it will never substitute for the realization of your own personal worth, particularly in the eyes of God. Accept your value as a multifaceted individual. Enjoy a rich variety of time investments. Open yourself to the range of joys available in work accomplishments, recreation, relationships, and spiritual growth.

Part V

DAILY
TOOLS

For Success with
Everyday Time Demands

DAILY
TOOLS

FOR SUCCESS WITH
EVERYDAY TIME DEMANDS

- Don't wait for a fix-everything, win-the-lottery solution.

- Gain big improvements with daily steps in the right direction.

Chapter 19

Early Excitement
Beats Running Late

*Peace I leave with you; My peace I give to you;
not as the world gives do I give to you.
Do not let your heart be troubled, nor let it be fearful.*
John 14:27 NASB

What's Ahead
- What works better than being on time.
- Cutting the chaos by picking the focal points.
- The thrill of working backwards.

Many people who are constantly late suffer real agonies trying to be on time. They want to meet their deadlines, get to the bus stop early, and avoid being the last to arrive for important meetings. But they feel they have so many demands that it's hopeless.

If this is one of your problem areas, take heart. You can learn some simple, effective techniques that will help you meet your commitments early, with time to spare.

Don't Try to Be on Time
Use your focus points to start designing a timetable that will help you meet your important commitments early. If you have

problems being late, don't just try to be on time. *Early* is the idea to concentrate on. Being on time is not enough; give yourself time to spare. It's a cushion against last-minute emergencies.

Pick Your Focus Points

Take a look at your weekly calendar. Select some important commitments you might not meet on time. Right now, choose only essentials. Once you've absorbed these techniques, you can easily use them for less important matters. Now let's take a look at a sample week's list.

Monday your department has its weekly staff meeting. Everyone reports on individual progress, and discusses departmental problems and objectives. You are often late, and you know it's not to your career advantage to acquire a reputation for lateness. Make this your first focus point.

Tuesday you have an employee counseling meeting that you're not looking forward to. Focus on this as something you are going to be early for this time.

Wednesday your monthly expense report is due. You haven't even begun to prepare it. It's always hard for you to get that report on your boss's desk on time. This is a good item to focus on.

Work Backwards

Let's apply the working backwards technique to that monthly expense report due Wednesday. You know your manager likes it on his desk by 3:00 P.M. Set a target of 2:30 so you'll have a half hour to check over the final draft and make copies. Working backwards, sort out the steps necessary to produce the finished report. Because you are just starting to use this tool, write the steps down to fix them in your mind. When it becomes second nature through practice, you'll be able to sort them out mentally. For now, you might write down:

- Finished report with three copies
- Overall total figures
- Total figures for individual categories

• Receipts arranged chronologically in separate categories

• All expense receipts assembled in one pile

Remember that large projects can be accomplished faster when they are divided into smaller, more manageable steps. For big jobs, estimate how long a step will take, total the time, and subtract from the target time. You will accomplish more when you give smaller steps a deadline. In fact, you may move ahead so quickly that you'll finish ahead of your timetable. Give yourself a double helping of congratulations when you do this. Invite someone who is interested in your efforts to overcome the lateness habit to congratulate you too.

Early Excitement Wins the Prize

You can design an effective timetable and stick to it more easily if you create excitement for being early and reward and reinforce your desirable behavior. This compensates for the storehouse of negative stimulation and excitement that being late offers. Know your Stimulation and Excitement Quota. Be creative in designing and delivering enough excitement to meet that quota. Make sure it exceeds the negative stimulation you got from being late.

For example, spend ten minutes reading that favorite mystery novel whenever you're ten minutes ahead of your schedule. Motivating yourself to be early is more important now than maintaining totally productive time. If you are ready to leave for work early, don't spend those extra minutes taking out the garbage; listen to some music you enjoy. Read your favorite psalms. Do something that is appealing and pleasurable. This rewards and reinforces your new behavior.

Jerry likes to memorize the Bible. He carries the sections he wants to learn to all his appointments. When he's early, he rewards himself by filling his mind with truth that lifts his spirit.

A busy executive with a large downtown bank departs for work 30 minutes earlier than he used to. He rewards himself by walking to the office. He enjoys the exercise, and he can think and plan as he strides briskly along. He arrives in a much more cheerful, productive frame of mind than he did when he used to squeeze himself onto a crowded, stuffy bus for a ten-minute ride every morning.

Reinforce positive behavior by reminding yourself what you gain by being early. Share your triumphs with someone on your support team who is interested in your progress.

Concentrate on Departure Time

Focusing on your departure time is another very useful technique for conquering the lateness habit. For example, if you have a meeting across town at 3:00 P.M., figure out what time you must leave your home or office to arrive there a few minutes early. Focus on that time.

Your calendar is particularly useful in such cases. As soon as you enter a meeting or commitment, write your departure time above it. If you need an extra reminder, circle the departure time in a bright color or put an asterisk or an "@" next to it. As you jot it down, take the thought one step further. Picture yourself leaving confidently at the appointed time. See yourself arriving at your destination calm and collected, with minutes to spare.

While you have your calendar in hand, also note what papers or materials you need for the meeting. If you can, take a few minutes to assemble those papers immediately. Tuck them into a file for that event. One man who always forgot important files now stacks them on the floor by his door at least an hour before departure.

Beware of the "one last thing" syndrome. Well before your departure, ask yourself, "If I were to do one last thing, what would it be?" Do it immediately or jot it in your calendar to do at a specific time.

Combine and Conquer

Now, let's use all these techniques for that Monday staff meeting. First, set a departure time. The meeting is at noon, and it will take five minutes to get to the tenth-floor conference room. Because the elevators are usually crowded at that time, give yourself an extra five minutes in case you have to wait for one. Enter and circle the departure time of 11:50 in your calendar. Then, work backwards and list the items you'll need:

- Notes on your projects.
- Memo from your boss on the department's monthly objectives.

Assemble the papers on Friday before you leave the office, or first thing Monday morning to avoid any last-minute preparations. Imagine how relaxed and confident you'll feel as you walk into that meeting on time and prepared.

Imitate the Early Birds

Learn from the Category One people who are habitually on time. Many won't be able to give you specific advice; they'll just say, "It's using common sense." But pay attention to their actions. How do they talk about departure time? How do they get themselves ready? Figure out how you can adapt their successful techniques to your own personal time management style. It's amazing how many useful ideas you can learn by studying people who have already mastered a sticky problem.

Track How Long Things Take

When Sarah raised her hand and volunteered to organize the missionary dinner, people around the table applauded. Sarah has the reputation of always being on time and always meeting the commitments she makes. But Sarah has a secret. She no longer tells people, because some have made fun of her. She always tracks how long things take. How long it takes to plan a dinner. How long the shopping will take. How many minutes to drive to church. How many minutes to get dressed and ready in the morning. She tracks everything, and she knows how to predict anything.

"It's exciting," she told a close friend. She loves to walk in the door a few minutes ahead of schedule, and she loves improving her time records. She gets more positive excitement from tracking and predicting the time than a colleague gets negative excitement from wandering along unaware and ending up late.

Share Sarah's secret. Track your time. Predict your time. Make it exciting to be early.

What's Really Behind Lateness

During the week, keep track of your own behavior. Analyze why and how you are late. Do you feel compelled to do "just one more thing"? Is it negative stimulation and excitement? Are you looking at every project as an enormous, time-consuming task rather than sorting it out into manageable steps?

Remember the secret payoffs of mismanaging time. Are you receiving attention, enjoying secret power, getting even with someone, or avoiding a certain feeling? Occasionally, deeper motivations may be involved. This was true in my case.

For years I struggled to be on time. Friends and colleagues frequently had to wait for me, sometimes on windswept street corners, and they were justifiably irritated. I recently learned that I made myself late habitually to avoid feeling abandoned.

The insight dawned one morning a few years ago, when I was scheduled to speak to a group of MBA candidates. On this occasion, I was ready ten minutes before a colleague was to come by and pick me up. It was a beautiful, sunny morning, so I waited outside. I stood feeling the warmth of the sun, enjoying the slight breeze, and congratulating myself on being early. I reveled in that ten minutes of rare early time, but when my colleague failed to show up at 8:00, I began to feel uneasy. By 8:10, I had looked at my watch at least 15 times. By 8:20, I began to feel frightened.

The feelings I was experiencing resembled the sinking sensation in the pit of my stomach that I used to have on dreaded occasions when I was in grammar school. When my classmates chose teams for softball games, I was usually the last one to be picked because I was nearsighted, shy, and overweight. I hated standing there alone until one of the team captains would say to the other, "You have to take her."

Years later, waiting in the sunshine, I was reliving those old feelings of being unwanted and left out. Suddenly, I realized that being late was a way of avoiding situations where I might feel that way again. Once I recognized my feelings, I could deal with this old fear more effectively.

If you are repeatedly late, there's probably a significant reason for your habit. Discover what it is. Allow yourself to understand what you gain. You will be able to change and deal with your time more effectively today.

Get There in Your Own Good Time

You can kick the lateness habit when you:

- Gear yourself to being early.
- Work backwards.
- Inject early excitement.
- Concentrate on departure time.
- Share Sarah's secret. Track your time.

Chapter 20

Yes Is a Time Trap When You Want to Say No

If God is for us, who can be against us?
Romans 8:31

What's Ahead

- How speaking the truth in love helps everyone.
- The right time to say no when people are close.
- How "plan and prevent" helps your time and your friends.

If you've had the experience of working with someone who says yes to requests he or she does not fulfill, you know how much time can be wasted. Deadlines are missed, work must be reassigned, and sometimes extra help must be hired to fill in at the last minute. In social situations, people accept invitations to parties they don't want to attend, run errands for family and friends when they really don't have time, and agree to take on volunteer duties they can't possibly cram into their schedules.

In a host of ways, many of us allow our precious time to be eaten away by demands we wish we could say no to. The trigger for this time waste comes in dozens of different ways. Do you say yes for any of these reasons?

- You don't want to hurt someone's feelings.

- You don't want to explain why you want to say no.

- You don't want to say anything that the other person might interpret as negative.

- You feel obligated to spend time with people because you haven't seen them recently.

- The other person is particularly important to you.

- You would really like to oblige, even though the timing is inappropriate.

Fortunately, there are proven tools to free you from the bind of saying yes when you don't want to, and help you learn how to say no skillfully and tactfully. They all relate to the big idea of speaking the truth in love.

> Instead, speaking the truth in love, we will in all things grow up into him who is the Head, that is, Christ (Ephesians 4:15).

Notice that Paul doesn't recommend "hinting the truth in love." He tells us to be "speaking the truth in love." So many times we feel that it's better to hint than speak, when hinting is actually confusing to others and tiring for us. So be careful about putting your message in behavior. Put it into skillful and truthful words with love.

Let's take a look at a typical family situation. It illustrates what can happen when someone learns to speak the truth in love.

Catch up on the Cleveland Crowd

Whenever John's older brother, Bud, came to town, it was a frustrating situation for John and his wife, Mary. Bud was the move-in-and-take-over type. John would get a call at the office and hear a hearty, "Hiya, kid! We're in town again! We'll be out for dinner around seven, okay? Got lots to tell you; good chance to get you caught up on the old crowd in Cleveland."

For years, John never had the heart to say no. He thought he owed it to his brother to be available; that Bud and Nancy would be hurt if he and Mary weren't hospitable. John and Mary would cancel their own plans and settle in for a long evening of catching up on Cleveland.

Over the years, a pattern developed. The call would come, Bud and Nancy would arrive for appetizers and conversation, they would all decide where to eat and then leave for the restaurant. After dinner, they'd return to John's for what Bud liked to refer to as a "real heart-to-heart." This might stretch out until after midnight. At that point John and Mary would ask Bud and Nancy to stay overnight, so more time was spent making up the guest room, getting out towels, finding pajamas, and so on. Then there was a "company breakfast" to prepare.

John and Mary finally decided to do something about Bud and his periodic invasions. It was time to "plan and prevent." First they defined what they wanted: a three- or four-hour leisurely dinner with relatives when they were in town. Then they defined what they didn't want: last-minute self-invitations that meant they had to rearrange their own plans at a moment's notice. With this in mind, John sat down and wrote the following note to his brother:

> Dear Bud,
>
> Great to see you last week, and fine to hear how things are going in Cleveland. Mary and I are both looking forward to your next visit. To make sure we don't have plans that will interfere with our getting together, will you give us a call a couple of weeks in advance? That way, we won't have to change plans, and we can make the reservations in advance and not have to cut into our time together.

Some months later, Bud flew into town in his usual fashion, called to surprise John, and ran head-on into a new brother. John and Mary had foreseen that Bud might "forget" to call ahead, so they'd practiced for just such an encounter.

In a firm but friendly manner, John explained that they had a previous commitment that would make it impossible for them to get together this time. "Listen, Bud," John wound up, "let's try for the next trip; just give me a call beforehand, and we should be able to arrange things."

Bud got the message. Next time, he called ahead. That's when Phase Two of John and Mary's plan went into gear. They wanted the evening to go smoothly, and they wanted to control their time.

When Bud called to announce his arrival, John suggested that they all meet at a particular restaurant. This eliminated the time previously spent at John's house, deciding where to eat and making reservations. It also meant that at the close of the meal, John and Mary were able to say good night and head home for a sensible bedtime.

Gradually, Bud and Nancy came to respect the new arrangements. This made it possible to vary the routine. John and Mary knew that they weren't locked into an extended visit every time. They could relax and enjoy hearing all the news from home in ways that had not been possible when they were seething with resentment under their dutiful family smiles.

A bonus for John and Mary was that they felt a lot better about their relatives. By learning how to say no, they made every yes an honest one.

"No" Isn't a Dirty Word

It's worthwhile to say no when you mean no because it benefits other people. The most considerate and thoughtful thing you can do for others is to spend time with them because you want to, not because you feel sorry, obligated, or trapped. Personal relationships built on pity have a rocky road ahead. Compassion for someone in real need is still an important basis for a service relationship. Joining your church convalescent hospital visitation program, assisting senior citizens who are hospitalized and have no families, and supporting Camp Fire activities or your local mental health association are certainly healthy and rewarding pursuits. But personal relationships that are totally one-way usually generate resentment and distance.

Check it out from your point of view. Would you want someone to spend time with you because they felt sorry for you or obligated? My hunch is that your answer is an immediate no. Consider it an absolute minimum of human decency to relate to other people because you want to be with them, not because you feel you "ought to."

Saying no also saves you both time and energy. Have you ever said to yourself, "Well, it's only one evening"? Follow up on that idea. There are seven evenings a week; "one evening" is a large percentage of your discretionary time. For people with demanding schedules, it could represent 100 percent of their available time for the week. Think carefully before using this rationalization for something you don't want to do.

Unintentional Rudeness

Saying no directly is a courtesy to other people. A "no" temporarily wrapped in a "yes" will crop up in indirect or confusing ways.

Peter and Eileen met each other during a coffee break at a seminar. There was an immediate and strong attraction, and for the next few months, they spent every possible minute together. Then Eileen began feeling uncomfortable and closed in, but she didn't tell Peter directly that she needed more time to herself. Instead, she showed her resentment in little, indirect ways— being late, losing things Peter had given her, and recognizing more of his weaknesses and pointing them out. When Peter asked her what was wrong, she quickly reassured him, "Everything is fine." But it wasn't. Peter felt confused. Eileen felt trapped. She would have saved them both time and bad feelings by saying no directly. If you don't take care of your own needs, you risk inadvertent rudeness to others.

"Yes" As a Barrier

Strange as it may seem, sometimes we don't say no when we want to because that kind of direct and open communication would open doors to closeness with others. If you spend obligation time with someone, it's easy to build up a wall of resentment between the two of you. Some of the most significant and satisfying moments in relationships occur when you give a thoughtful and considerate no.

Rx for Saying No

Learning how to say no when you want to depends on increasing:

- your self-respect
- your confidence about relying on your own standards and decisions
- your recognition that you are not responsible for others' feelings
- your understanding that your worth does not depend on other people's judgments
- your comfort and confidence in taking care of yourself

It's challenging to integrate this prescription into your time program, but each step forward can help you learn when and how to say no.

Step 1: Pick one relationship or type of situation where you've said yes inappropriately several times during the past three or four months. Concentrate on this developmental area first. Pray about it. See what the Bible says about the situation.

Step 2: Discover your motivation for saying yes. Are you trying to please someone? Are you concerned that saying no might injure the relationship? Are you worried about the other person's feelings?

Step 3: Ask yourself when the problem is likely to recur. Is it associated with the weekend? With holidays? With a particular time of day?

Step 4: Put together a plan of action for preventing this next time. Part of this step involves preparing yourself for the occasion. Another part involves preventing the occasion from recurring.

In terms of preparation, you may need to remind yourself several times that your worth does not depend on other people's judgments. Tell yourself, "I don't need to please everyone. I only need to please Jesus."

In the prevention category, we come back to the idea of directness. If someone asks you out and you do not plan to accept the invitation, it's both fair and thoughtful to let that person know that in some way. Here is what one woman did.

The third time Debra was asked out by a colleague she liked but did not want to date, she decided to be more specific.

"Rob, it means a lot to me to work with you, and I want our good working relationship to continue. I appreciate you asking me to dinner, but dating isn't right for me. We have an important friendship. And what do you think of the new project our team just got?"

Step 5: Practice your new response. Get in touch with how you sound and feel as you say no in a skillful and thoughtful way. Practice with someone who has good judgment and isn't involved in the situation. You'll be delighted by the ease with which the right words will come to your lips when you've invested the time in practicing. It may not feel natural at first, but it will feel better with practice.

Your personal integrity and worth do not depend on pleasing everyone. These qualities are enhanced by pleasing God. Use your time in a way that enables you to say without question, "I did what was right for me. Other people may be doing things I disagree with, but I am only responsible for me."

Some people may choose to feel hurt no matter what you do. Taking the time to understand and accept your own standards is comforting when you run into someone who wants you to feel guilty. Listen for signals of guilt being offered. The phrase, "If it weren't for you, I..." is often the envelope that bears an invitation for guilt. Recognize these early warning signals and quickly decline invitations of unrealistic guilt.

Parents and Children

It's a real challenge to know when and how to say no to the people close to you. It's easy to feel guilty when a parent complains, "But you never call me!" or a child says, "If you really loved me, you'd get it for me." The first thing to do is give yourself some time and pray. Find what biblical principles apply. Ask God for guidance. Talk with people of good character. Then to find the best solution for everyone involved, get some perspective on what people really want from you. For parents and children alike, it's most often simply a need to have you reaffirm your love and affection for them.

Think how easy it would be to give that kind of affirmation to your parents in brief but frequent phone calls. You could sandwich calls in once a week while you're preparing dinner, before you settle down to read for the evening, early in the morning, or before you go to work. A warm, "Hi, Mom, just called to say I love you and I'm thinking about you," can work wonders. "Dad, I thought of you today when I saw the sunrise. I'm so glad to be your son," is a way to tell your father that you love and honor him.

The same principle will work with children. Marilyn, a working single parent, reported that she spent less time fussing about saying no to her four- and six-year-olds when she made looking each son in the eyes and telling him, "I love you" every day one of her Central Concerns.

Take the time to do what is important. You'll have a better basis for saying no when you need to.

You Want/I Want Mix and Match

Always know what you want before you decide to say yes. You won't always be able to do what you want or get what you want, but you will make better decisions and take more considerate action if you have this information before you make your decision. Don't stop yourself from knowing what you want by saying things like "I could never do that" or "It just wouldn't be right."

Clarifying what other people really want can save you time and energy and still enable them to get everything they want.

Maria was active in her volunteer youth group. She did it because she wanted to, but she dreaded the annual mint sale. All the leaders were expected to open up their car trunks, stack in 30 or 40 cases of mints, and sell them. She had wanted to say no for the last two years, but felt obligated because it was for such a good cause. This year, when the mint sale drive opened, she realized that what the organization really wanted was a contribution to their budget. She found out how much profit each box brought in, then wrote a check for the amount her allotment of mints would have contributed to the group.

Another member of the executive board used a different tactic. The group did not necessarily expect board members to sell the mints; they just wanted the money for the group. So he gave his trunk load of mints to a nephew who worked in a tennis club, and the 40 cases of mints were sold in a record two days. Clarify what people want, know what you want, and explore creative ways of achieving both.

Do not allow yourself to fall into the pit of "feeling obligated" for a favor from a friend. Assume that other people do things for you because they want to. If you have potential problems in this area, clarify your stance immediately. Say something like, "Mary, I know you are doing a great deal for me, and I appreciate it. It's important for me to know that you aren't doing anything because of a sense of obligation. Only do it if you want to." When you have this kind of understanding, you won't drag yourself down with obligation.

"No" Is a Word to Live By

Stop saying yes to people because you believe a no will hurt their feelings. Contrary to what you may feel, this isn't thoughtful. In reality, it means that you don't think they have enough personal integrity, strength, and intelligence to manage their own lives. Considered in perspective, it's almost as though you told them, "You poor, weak thing. I know you can't take care of yourself. Even if I don't really want to, I will take on the burden of caring for you because I feel sorry for you." Not very flattering, is it? And it's not truthful. Give people the same respect you want them to give you. Most want to stand on their own two feet and face life directly. Help them by developing these techniques for saying no. It will pay off for you both. You'll get even more from your time with people when you:

- Plan ways to prevent the unwilling "yes."

- Prepare yourself to say no with courtesy and skill.

- Practice your responses ahead of time.

- Say yes when it helps others get what they want and helps you get what you want.

When you are tempted to say yes when you know you should say no, keep these powerful words in front of you: Speak the truth in love.

Chapter 21

How to Never Waste
a Moment Waiting Again

He that handleth a matter wisely shall find good.
Proverbs 16:20 KJV

What's Ahead

- What has to be in place for this high-payoff tool to work.
- An often overlooked place to find more time.
- Practical and surprising ideas to help you transform time wasted waiting.

Waiting is a growing problem. When other people are careless about time, it cuts into your time and energy. Those of us who have managed to avoid the lateness syndrome still have to deal with it in others, and we're all familiar with the frustrations of waiting. We may complain about it, but a solution often seems elusive.

However, a great way to turn waiting time into useful time is the big idea for this chapter: Use the crumbs. Put small sections of time to work for big purposes.

Time In and Time Out Come First

Before you can transform time wasted waiting, make sure you have allowed yourself the right balance of productive Time In and restful Time Out. If you are pushing yourself all the time with no Time Out, it's easy to forget your resolve, grab a junk magazine, reach for the potato chips, and hide out for the evening. To help you remember Time In or Time Out, think of a light switch that is totally on or totally off. Few people can or want to be totally "on" all the time. Having a good balance of Time Out gives you more energy for Time In, and you'll find yourself wanting to turn those crumbs of waiting time into time you value.

Use the Crumbs

See what a difference these practical and surprising steps make:

1. Keep your written weekly and daily targets in mind

When you have written weekly targets of things you want to accomplish this week, you will be amazed how you can use those crumbs of waiting time. You may write a thank-you note you have listed, call a sick friend, call a store to check if the paint for the chair you are refinishing is in stock, or study for the Spanish class you are taking. Written weekly and daily targets focus you and lift your creativity to a new level.

2. Unplug the television

You might ask what your TV has to do with waiting. Turning on the TV is often optional waiting time for something useful or restful to appear. Skip it, and you gain an amazing amount of time and energy.

For years, if you were to walk into my home, you would not see a television. Then life changed to having a television. Gradually, a new habit developed—turning on the television to relax. What a waste and drain, but I still did it. Then I unplugged it.

Needing to make that extra mental motion of plugging it in made me more conscious of the time. Here's what happened. Unplugging the TV cut out images that displeased God and contaminated my mind. Unplugging speeded up activities like cooking or kitchen cleanup that used to include having the TV on for background. Unplugging gave me opportunities to fill my mind with things that gave me a lift, wisdom, and a smile.

3. Turn waiting time into memorizing time

You may say, "You don't know the lines I have to wait in." That's true, I don't. But I do know the lift that comes from turning your mind to memorizing quotes from the Bible whenever waiting. My driving time is different since turning stalled-in-heavy-traffic time into memorizing and thinking about this quote on love:

> Love is patient and kind; it is not jealous or conceited or proud; love is not ill-mannered or selfish or irritable; love does not keep a record of wrongs; love is not happy with evil, but is happy with the truth. Love never gives up; and its faith, hope, and patience never fail. Love is eternal (1 Corinthians 13:4-8 TEV).

While brushing your teeth and putting on makeup are not exactly waiting time, they are also great times to memorize or listen to the Bible on a tape recorder. Consider putting a small recorder with tapes of the Bible into your bathroom. You will be pleased at how it calms your heart and focuses your mind.

Brag to Someone

This high-return tool for turning waiting time into positive and productive time requires a big change for most people. If it is something you want to do, but are concerned that you might let your resolve slip, pray about it. If it is the right thing for you to do, use it to motivate yourself. Find a brag buddy. Give account to a caring and supportive person on a daily basis. You will be pleased at how a short accountability phone call once a day helps your commitment.

If you were to visit Claire on a Saturday night, you would usually find her sitting at her dining table with a determined look, a big smile, and small cards spread out in front of her. Claire loves winning the challenge she has with a Sunday morning accountability partner for memorizing the Bible. On Sunday morning over coffee, her partner will finger Claire's collection of cards with quotes from the Bible and pull out only one. Claire's challenge is to repeat the verse word by word from her heart.

Even though Claire's busy week includes managing a medical laboratory, concerts, and community service, she turns any spare moments during the week to filling her heart with the Bible, and she turns her Saturday evenings to spreading out the cards with quotes and getting her mind and heart ready for the accountability challenge.

You don't have to be inflexible about this tool. Just be as accountable to your brag buddy as you need to in order for it to be effective.

Work Out a Plan B

If you analyze your waiting periods, you'll probably discover that they fall into patterns. Anticipate and prepare for these possible problem areas.

George's boss was notorious for running late on appointments with his staff. George felt that cooling his heels with the rest of the gang waiting to enter the inner sanctum wasn't appropriate. The company was the loser if he did because that kind of waiting wasn't productive. He devised a better way to deal with this chronic problem.

Whenever George has an appointment with his boss, he is fully prepared by departure time, but he doesn't leave his office without calling ahead to find out if the boss is on schedule. If his boss is running late, George asks the assistant to buzz him when the preceding appointment is ending. When he receives the signal, he leaves immediately. During his waiting time, George deals with tasks that don't require serious concentration, so he can drop them quickly. He reviews his calendar, jots down phone calls to make later in the day, handles routine email, or checks his current reading file to catch up on industry news.

If you find yourself in a similar situation, but can't spend your waiting time in your office, there's an alternative solution. Take some portable work with you to the appointment, and do it while you're waiting. It could be an article you want to read, a report you want to edit, or some figures you want to go over.

Consider the Day-Before Call

Explore the habit of confirming appointments the day before. It takes only two or three minutes to call, and if you avoid one no-show or mix-up a week, it's well worth your time.

Eliminate What You Can

Consciously aim to eliminate or reduce waiting time every week. For example, consider an area like personal services. Do you spend time waiting to get your hair cut? Do you have to wait for the dentist regularly, even though you have a firm appointment? What about getting your car serviced? There are so many areas where we can't reduce or eliminate waiting time that it pays to explore every area where we can.

First, consider finding another supplier for the personal service. If you can't solve the problem this way, there are other techniques that can reduce or eliminate waiting time.

You have a noon appointment with the dentist and your departure time is 11:30. Before you set out, phone the dentist's office to check if he or she is running on time. If not, ask when the dentist will be ready to see you and adjust your departure time accordingly.

If your staff meetings have been running late for weeks because one person always barges in twenty minutes late, you could let the chairperson know your feelings directly. "The last four meetings ran overtime because they didn't begin on schedule. This is creating a lot of time pressures for me. Will you let people know the meetings will begin on the dot of the appointed hour and then go ahead and start, even if everyone hasn't arrived? I'll support you enthusiastically if you take this action."

You can often wipe out waiting time when you let people know directly and tactfully what you want.

Don't Expect People to Read Your Mind

When you are hosting a dinner party or social gathering, you may sometimes find yourself waiting for everyone to leave. It was a wonderful party, but now the evening is on the wane. You want to clean up and do the dishes before midnight, but your guests linger on.

Surprisingly, telling your guests when to go home is one of the most gracious things you can do as a host. Many people find it difficult to be the first to leave a party and welcome leadership in this area.

One technique is to begin talking about the evening in the past tense. "It was so nice to see you all. I hope we can get together again soon. It was such fun to have you over."

Another alternative is to let people know the approximate departure time when you invite them. "Could you come for dessert from seven to nine?"

Monty decided he wanted his evening social engagements to end by 10:00 P.M. If he's at someone else's house, he thanks his host and leaves. If he has guests in his own house, he goes to a nearby light switch at 10:00 and switches it off and on. His friends kid him, but they know that's the signal for "good night." New acquaintances are sometimes a bit surprised, but Monty does it with such a pleasant and reasonable smile that they accept it. Many secretly admire his style. And there's no doubt about where he stands.

Win the Twenty-Fifth Hour

We can't eliminate all daily waiting time, but we can learn to use it creatively and productively. Part of the secret lies in your attitude. Imagine waiting time as precious minutes in the magical "twenty-fifth" hour.

Maria works for a large Midwestern department store chain. She gets so much done that she's often been kidded about finding a twenty-fifth hour from somewhere. She told me she has a secret. She uses every second to her advantage. If she has to wait for a taxi, she mentally reviews her time for the next day and groups any related commitments and objectives. She may realize that her 3:00 P.M. appointment will put her in the same building as her lawyer. He'd asked her to drop by next time she was in the area to sign a couple of papers, so she can group this errand with the other appointment. Her 11:00 A.M. meeting is being held near her favorite Italian restaurant, so she can phone a friend to invite her there for lunch.

By looking ahead and noting patterns, she is able to group individual tasks into efficient time blocks. She's also better prepared to deal with any waiting time that could crop up. The minutes she gains add up to that magical "twenty-fifth" hour.

Waiting Time Can Be Wonderful

To highlight how to turn those crumbs of waiting time into satisfying and rewarding time, consider:

- Prepare your attitude. Allow yourself the right amount of Time In and Time Out so you will feel like using the waiting time to good purpose.

- Have your written target in mind and probably in hand to inspire your focus.

- Unplug the television.

- Turn waiting time into memorizing time and give your spirit and mind a lift.

- Most of all, use the crumbs of time for what is important to you.

You can use the next chapter to help you handle interruptions without hurt feelings.

Chapter 22

Interruptions—Coping Without Being Rude

*I have learned the secret of being content in any and every situation....
I can do everything through him who gives me strength.*
Philippians 4:12,13

What's Ahead

• Finding ways for handling interruptions that benefit both parties.

• How hinting and hoping drains time and confuses people.

• How communicating directly now prevents complaining later.

Let's examine the most common reason interruptions are a challenge—the fear that if you take care of your time needs, you hurt the people in your life. It's concern about a win-lose teeter-totter. What's better is finding ways where both people win. This means turning a one-benefit teeter-totter into a both-benefit table. Rather than feeling that if you help yourself, you automatically lower the other person, find a solution that benefits and lifts you both.

When you think of John and Charles Wesley, you probably think of a great heritage of hymns or a powerful spiritual awakening. You probably don't think of the interruptions their mother must have faced as she reared her household full of children. How easy it would be for someone in her situation to say, "I have too many interruptions. I can't pray." Yet she found a way to handle interruptions that helped her and her children. A famous story of Susanna Wesley shares how she sat at her kitchen table with an apron over her head to tell all her children when she needed time to pray without interruption. That had to be a both-benefit solution. I'm sure her children knew that life in the Wesley house would be better after their mother's prayer time.

Most of us are not willing to pursue our own objectives selfishly without considering other people. We don't like to tell friends or coworkers that their visits, calls, or conversation may be an unwelcome interruption at that moment. Whenever I speak about time, this concern is always on the tip of someone's tongue: "But I don't want to hurt their feelings." "I wouldn't have any friends." "You can't say that to the people I'm with. They just wouldn't understand." These are all valid concerns, and they are based on our regard for other people. Unfortunately, these concerns often backfire.

Consider what we see about the character of God in the words of Jesus:

> Ask and it will be given to you; seek and you will find; knock and the door will be opened to you. For everyone who asks receives; he who seeks finds; and to him who knocks, the door will be opened (Matthew 7:7,8).

This section of Scripture is bursting with direct communication. I've looked for examples to support the style of hinting and hoping, but I have learned the hinting and hoping habit has a frequent side effect—complaining to others.

When we don't take the more loving and harder step of communicating directly, have you noticed how easy it is to complain to others or seethe to ourselves? When you communicate directly and skillfully, you clean out the temptation to complain to others, and you stop stuffing feelings that often blow up in arguments. You also handle interruptions and an array of other awkward situations in much less time.

Inconsiderate or Just Unaware

Most people want to help you with your time. They want to respect it, but they may stay too long, talk at the wrong time, or interrupt you when you are concentrating on a rush project. They don't do it deliberately. They simply get carried away by their own enthusiasm or lack of knowledge about the pressures you are facing.

Here's a personal example. After an enjoyable breakfast with a friend at a neighborhood café, I stopped by her house to admire a massive oak chest that she had refinished. As I continued to chat, she said something I really appreciated.

"I'm feeling pressured about the shopping I need to do for the family today. I had a lovely breakfast with you, and now I need to be moving on to my chores." Her directness adds pleasure to my time with her. I have the comfort of knowing that when we're together, it's because she wants to be there. I'm never on edge wondering if I've overstayed my welcome.

One man endeared himself to a special single lady in his life by checking whenever he called with, "Am I calling at a good time for you?" She said that his thoughtfulness communicated care in a way flowers alone could not.

Communicate Directly and Skillfully

Take the time to let others know directly the pressures you're under and the deadlines you face. Learn to do it with tact and skill. Others do appreciate us more when we maintain a healthy amount of concern about feelings, and at the same time mix in thoughtful communication skills.

Some people don't believe this. They share the sentiment expressed by a young physician: "I shouldn't have to tell colleagues when I'm busy. They should know I don't have time to talk when I keep my pen in hand, poised over a stack of papers." That's not direct enough. It's not efficient and thoughtful.

If a friend is rhapsodizing about her new house, and you appear distant or indifferent because you're worrying about leaving for an appointment you haven't mentioned, she's likely to start questioning your friendship. You could save hours of explanation and apology by telling her immediately that you're rushed and that you'd like to talk about her new house as soon as you get back. Then she knows that you're interested in what she has to say, and won't have reason to misunderstand your preoccupation.

Add a Dash of Diplomacy

There are several direct and courteous ways to let others know that you don't have time to chat without running the risk of hurt feelings.

You might say, "Your weekend trip to Miami sounds great. It's certainly more appealing than the project I'm working on right now." Or, "I'm pleased about your new marketing plan. Right now I'm just so distracted by the noon deadline that's coming up that I'm not concentrating on you as much as I'd like to."

One woman found that reaching out to touch a talkative friend lightly on the arm was a tactful way to get her to pause in the conversation. Then she could explain that she was working on a deadline and wouldn't be able to talk until later.

What about the people who take up your time on the phone? Remember, they can't see that you are surrounded by anxious people and in imminent danger of being crushed by a tottering stack in your in-basket. It's only courteous to let them know the pressure you're under at the moment. You might say, "I'm glad you called, Jim. Catching up on the news with you is always a lift. If I had my way, I'd put my feet up and talk with you and forget this stack of work. But I think I had better keep plowing through it. I'm glad you called and that we had a minute to touch base."

The Right Tone

Even the most tactful comment will not work if the tone of your voice, facial gestures, and posture do not convey respect and care. You probably know someone who uses all the right phrases, but really believes that people are shabby excuses for using up oxygen. Skillful phrases add to respect; they do not substitute for it.

Many times the reasons for trouble with interruptions aren't because of attitude; they are because of a lack of practical tools. Let's look at seven ideas.

Tools to Help You Find Solutions That Are of Mutual Benefit

These tools go to the top of the popularity list for both men and women:

1. Say yes to the person and no to the request

You can say yes to the person and also say no to the request. You do this by affirming the individual without agreeing to the time investment.

Saying yes to the person and no to the request starts before you open your mouth. It means mentally reminding yourself that you are not rejecting the person. You are declining the request.

Jay could say no on the job, but he turned into a marshmallow at home. Although going to the ballet was number 98 on his list of "100 Things I Could Do," he'd always say yes when his wife would ask him to go. Yet he was happy to say yes to coaching his daughter's soccer team, being on the fund-raising committee for basketball uniforms for his son, and building the new fence that his wife wanted in their backyard.

He started reminding himself that he could say yes to the person and no to the request. He stopped doing the things he had previously accepted but resented. His telephone calls started sounding more like this, "It's good to hear your voice. It sounds as though you are busy on these events for the school. Because I am already scheduled for four parent activities, I am going to let this one pass." He learned to show respect for the person and his cause without feeling a need to take on the new cause.

Jay even took his wife out for a leisurely cup of coffee and her favorite macadamia nut chocolate chip cookie, told her how much he loved her, and asked if there was some other way he could show her his love besides going to the ballet.

You may not need the coffee and chocolate chip cookie strategy, but here are two possibilities to help you say yes to the person in a way that suits your style and still says no to the request:

- "It's great to hear your voice and to find out what you are doing. Right now, I'm volunteering for visitations at convalescent hospitals, so I'm going to let this opportunity go. And I certainly congratulate you on what you are doing and I'm going to tell a friend about it."

- "I'm always interested in hearing what you have in mind. Let me make sure I understand what you are wanting." Then paraphrase what you heard the person asking for and why. This is a great time to pray in your heart as you listen. If you have heard, and it isn't something that is right for you to be involved in, then continue with something like this: "What you are asking is important, and yet it's not the right thing for me to be giving to right now; however, I will pray for this cause whenever God brings it to my mind."

If you are tempted to say that none of the above suggestions will work for you, the exact wording may not work, but the principle will. Experiment with it. Tailor the wording to your personality and situation, practice it, and then test it. You both benefit. You'll feel better when you are honest from the start, and the other person will know that you care. I think you will be pleased with how you save time now and resentment later by saying yes to the person and no to the request.

2. Share with people, "I need to check my calendar"

Betty said it still amazed her that people responded to this simple statement with such understanding. The first time Betty was going to use her new technique, she knew that her neck had red splotches, and that her heart beat faster, and that her face was flushed. But she went ahead and used her technique, and to her surprise, the other person answered with a smile and said, "Fine."

Sometimes the simplest techniques are the most effective.

3. "I'll get back to you before noon tomorrow"

Marci had struggled to say no for years before she finally found the technique that brought her success. People always seemed to understand when she told them, "I have several things pending on my calendar right now. I will let you know before noon tomorrow."

Marci knew that between the time of the request and noon tomorrow, she would be able to sit down with a yellow pad and write down her pros and cons. She could then sit up straight and talk herself into the right response—usually a "no."

Marci even taped a sticker to her telephone, "I'll let you know before noon tomorrow."

Why include, "I'll get back to you before noon tomorrow"? It lets people know when they can expect an answer. It lets them know you are not brushing them off forever. And it lets them know not to call you back in four hours.

4. Get the specifics

Take some time to find out whether this is a two-minute or a two-hour interruption. Can it be handled later or by someone else? Does the interruption mask another need?

Plus, the more specifics you have about when people interrupt you, why they interrupt you, and who interrupts you, the easier it is to prevent problems in the future.

Getting the specifics helps you let the other person know that you care and that you hear their concern.

Getting the specifics helps you see how to make the interruption contribute to one of your priorities.

Getting the specifics helps you help the other person get what they really want.

5. Have available times

Let people know when you are available to be interrupted.

Certain people are in their office or near their telephone and reachable between 8 and 9 A.M., and between 4 and 5 P.M. Once people know when you are most available, they will concentrate on contacting you during that time.

You probably know someone, a CPA or an attorney, for whom you can leave messages all day, but you know you will get your call returned between a window of time they have established to protect their schedule. It's a great example to follow.

6. End with preventing interruptions

Prevent problems by giving yourself a checkpoint at the end of the conversation. Stop for a moment to summarize what's been covered. Ask yourself, and perhaps the other person, if there is anything else that might crop up that hasn't been discussed. Tie up loose ends during that time to look back and look ahead to prevent future interruptions.

7. Anticipate

"Oh, no; tomorrow is my wife's birthday, and I have to get her something."

When Randy said this to his friend over lunch, he was shocked to hear his friend respond, "How can you be surprised about your wife's birthday? You've had 365 days to shop for exactly the right present for her."

Reduce the number of interruptions by anticipating. If you are surprised the day before a person's birthday, start predicting when a surprise could come up. Many people are amazed at the accuracy they can bring to this task. They can look at their calendar for the next month and actually predict what surprises might be dropping into their lives. Because his friend razzed him so much, Randy has even put together a page with all his "gift events" and dates to remember for the entire year.

Because interruptions are a part of most people's lives, the secret is to use the tools and then get back on track quickly.

Respect Your Own Time

Concern for others can certainly complicate time. Learn to use the techniques in this chapter to balance this concern with the respect your own time deserves. Tell people directly what your time frame is; ask what pressures they are facing. As you build and practice these skills, you'll have more time to achieve your objectives and help those around you to achieve theirs. You will be showing concern for others in new ways.

Time—A Rich Resource

You can find ways to handle interruptions well. You don't have to put an apron over your head like Susanna Wesley did, but you can use her style of finding something that benefits you and other people.

- Turn a teeter-totter into a table. Turn a situation where one person wins into one where both benefit.

- Continually find new ways to help your friends, family, and work associates give your time the respect it deserves.

- Communicate directly and skillfully.

- Experiment with the seven interruption techniques.

Allow time to be a rich resource for all of us to enjoy even with the phone ringing.

Chapter 23

The Telephone—Tool or Tyrant?

*Do not let any unwholesome talk come out of your mouths,
but only what is helpful for building others up according to
their needs, that it may benefit those who listen.*

Ephesians 4:29

What's Ahead

- How a leadership hat helps you with the telephone.
- Why communicating directly is so important on the phone.
- When telephone time can be turned into prayer time.

As I looked into the office of a retired Marine Corps general who headed a division where I was working on a special project, he motioned for me to sit down as he finished his phone call. He was focused on the phone. He was direct. He was clear as he summed up the call. And he sounded as though he was still wearing a general's hat and uniform. As I had a chance to work with him, he demonstrated the secret for keeping the telephone a tool and not a tyrant. It's the same tool I have seen a mother of three use standing by her kitchen phone. When you pick up the phone, be a leader. Wear your leadership hat even though it probably doesn't look like the same one on the head of a Marine Corps general.

Even with all the communications that are now funneled into email, people still share how they feel pressured by the phone. It's more personal. It's more invasive. And it's hard to delete your talkative neighbor even if you have work piled up to your shoulders.

Let's look at some practical ways to handle this potential problem.

What's Eating Up Your Telephone Time?

If you feel your time is being eaten up by the telephone, first learn where your time is going.

Ask yourself these questions about each call you make or receive during the next five days. Write your answers in your Time Notebook:

1. With whom did you talk?

2. Who initiated the call?

3. What was covered?

4. What was achieved?

Your notes can lead to some valuable insights. Most people discover that it's rarely everyone they know who wastes their time on the telephone. Typically, it's a small group of people. Sometimes, people discover that they themselves initiate the time-wasting calls.

Paul handled finance management for a chain of sporting good stores. He realized that although he complained about his time on the phone, he really liked it. "Most of my work is very isolated. Consequently, when I become tired working only with figures, I start finding telephone calls I just have to make."

Know what you get from your telephone time. You may discover that phone interruptions are really sources of excitement and stimulation. Before you give up the phone calls, substitute something more positive. Or decide to accept your need for stimulation and work out ways to make your phone calls more productive and satisfying.

Next, come to grips with the question, "What was covered?" When you're jotting down your notes, be aware of how much time was spent talking about the weather and other topics of casual conversation.

What you achieved during the telephone conversation is the next consideration. Returning a call is not an achievement; it's an activity. You may find that your time is wasted because people call you without leaving a complete message. When you call back, you don't know the objective of the call. Keeping track of what was achieved gives you an easier way of determining necessary changes.

Speak Right Up—Say What You Want

Before you place a telephone call, decide specifically what you want to accomplish. Jot down two or three items on your calendar or notepad and then check them off as you cover them during the call. If it's a personal call, reaffirm your objective to "make contact." Knowing what you want to accomplish lets you know when you're through.

The Same Old Numbers

Your notes can also help you spot recurring problems. For instance, do many of your phone calls result from your inability to meet deadlines? Do your coworkers and supervisors call for explanations of delays? Do you have to make a lot of calls to get extensions on the deadline, or explain why the expected report won't be ready until next Tuesday? In such a case, the phone is not the problem; your difficulty in meeting deadlines is.

Do you have friends or relatives who constantly call for no specific reason, engaging you in time-consuming chats about nothing important? Maybe they are feeling neglected. They may want to be reassured that you still value them. You might eliminate those irritating interruptions by setting aside a few minutes at regular intervals to call them and initiate a chat. Help satisfy their needs but do it at a time that's best for you.

Make the Best Connection—Be Considerate

Be considerate of others when you call them. It only takes a couple of seconds to ask, "Is this a convenient time for you to talk?" Those few seconds can make such a difference for you. If it is not convenient for the other person, you won't be getting his or her full attention. Work out a phrase that fits your time-management style. Use it when you call others. It may encourage them to be more considerate of your time.

When people phone you, it's also important to be considerate. Let them know if you are under pressure rather than merely giving them your divided attention. Because this is a difficult area for many people, have several expressions ready that you can use if this occurs. For example:

"I have a rush project on my desk right now, and I would like to call you back this afternoon. Will that work for you?"

"I'm enjoying our conversation, but I have some urgent deadlines on my mind. May I call you back tomorrow?"

"I have company right now. When can I call you back tomorrow?"

If you let people rattle on when it's not convenient, you're not really doing them a favor or being polite. If you allow them to impose on your time before you tell them it's not convenient to talk, they are going to feel embarrassed and annoyed. So do everyone a favor. Learn to say, "May I call you back later?" in whatever manner best suits your style and situation.

Get a Good Start—Lead the Conversation

Start your conversation quickly and skillfully. Your tone of voice can carry warmth and respect. Five minutes of conversation about the football game or some other routine topic is not a necessary warm-up. Most people appreciate it when you take the time to think out what you want to accomplish with a phone call and get to the point right away. It saves their time as well as yours. Handled courteously and in a friendly tone, the telephone is usually a welcome conduit for conducting business and enjoying your friends and family.

How to Say Goodbye and Hang Up

In a business setting particularly, it is appropriate for either person to signal the close of the call when business is completed. Talking about the call in the past tense is an effective way to close the conversation gently.

"It sounds like we've wrapped up most of the issues. Is there anything else we need to talk about before we close the call?"

"I'm glad you called. It has been good checking over these items before the meeting."

"I'm glad we've had this opportunity to bring each other up to date. It's been good talking with you."

The Needy Friend and the 90-Minute Calls

Natalie found herself squeezed for time by a friend who had a difficult childhood, a difficult situation today, and a love of talking on the phone. Her friend told her over and over about her mother, who would control the family at home by having them tiptoe around her and reminding them that they could give her a heart attack. When Natalie's friend calls and "needs to talk now," it can take up to 90 minutes of listening.

After Natalie had listened and prayed with her friend repeatedly, she finally decided on a different plan. Natalie now calls her friend two mornings a week to pray with her. They spend 10 minutes in prayer each time. Then Natalie turns on her answering machine and continues her work. She picks up messages frequently and returns them at the beginning of the morning, at noon, and in the early evening. When her friend leaves a message, Natalie prays then and prays again during their next regular prayer call.

People Come First

Stay in touch with the reality that the telephone is only a tool. By giving it power over your time, you are the one who makes it a tyrant. No matter how important the phone may seem, remember that people come first. Use it skillfully, and it will enhance your time and your life.

- Remember to wear your leadership hat.
- Tell people what you want directly.
- Be considerate—make the best connection.
- Take hold of the conversation at the start.
- Develop tact and skill in closing a call.

Part VI

Spiritual Tools

*For Enjoying Your
Coach and Counselor*

SPIRITUAL TOOLS

FOR ENJOYING YOUR COACH AND COUNSELOR

🕊 Clean out the idea that spiritual growth is climbing a ladder to God.

🕊 Accept the gift of a loving relationship with God and grow in His love and power.

Chapter 24

Put PBC on
Your Calendar

He will be called Wonderful Counselor,
Mighty God, Everlasting Father, Prince of Peace.
Isaiah 9:6

Have you ever had your head on your pillow in the morning, heard the alarm rattle, and started for the shower when all of a sudden you are thinking about a tough situation that you will have to handle sometime soon? Even before you can step into the shower, the situation has lurched into the middle of your mind.

Perhaps the situation is confronting a son or daughter about something you have found. Perhaps it is letting an employee go. Perhaps it is confronting your manager. Perhaps it is confronting a trusted friend. Perhaps it is a business commitment that has gone sour.

Whatever the situation is, it's easy to imagine putting your head back on the pillow for a few more minutes and hoping that situation will somehow go away.

But you know it won't be going anywhere.

At this point, you face two big choices. Try and handle it alone. Or face it with your Coach—your "Wonderful Counselor."

Whether you try to go it alone or whether you ask for God's guidance, strength, and help in the situation depends on your relationship with Him. If you have been ignoring God much of the time, you are likely to try and do it alone.

On the other hand, if you have been using three powerful keys to building your relationship with God, you are likely to turn to God.

The first of the three keys is simple yet powerful, and it unlocks the door to not only handling your time pressures more effectively, but to enjoying more love, joy, and peace in your time.

Put "PBC" on Your Calendar Daily

In this formula P stands for praying, B stands for reading the Bible, and C stands for seeking to know more of the character of God as you read the Bible. Being able to put PBC on your calendar will give you more focus, closure, and energy.

"P" for Praying

> Our Father in heaven... (Matthew 6:9).

Because prayer is talking with God, it's easy to see how important this is in building a relationship with Him. For a moment, look at the relationship from a different side. Imagine being in a room with someone to whom you have given many gifts at a great price and that person runs around doing things with those gifts, yet never says a word to you.

At the very least, this action would distance the relationship. And that's what we do when we don't talk with God. In addition, we miss His guidance and power. So the key is to remember that you can talk with Him about anything and everything, and you can do it anytime. In the psalms we are told that God turns to hear us:

> I waited patiently for the LORD: he turned to me and heard my cry (Psalm 40:1).

Prayer didn't always have such a central place in my heart. After being single most of my life I married—you guessed it—

an orderly Category One. Before our wedding, I told him I was a Category Two, but he didn't believe it then.

Times changed when I married this wonderful widower with three teenage children and moved from a quiet condominium in San Francisco to a busy house in the suburbs. When marriage and stepchildren did not deliver my dream of romance and happiness, one night I sought out my friend Elizabeth, who had helped me investigate the Bible and trust Jesus, and pleaded, "Is there any biblical way out of this marriage?"

My life took a different turn when she took me by the hand, looked me in the eyes, and explained, "No. There is no biblical way out of your marriage. You are about to become a woman of prayer."

This unexpected response opened the door to the healing power of prayer, the joy of faith, and the surprise of abundant time in my life.

My story of how God can heal a marriage through prayer plus practical steps for becoming a person of prayer are summarized in *The Prayer Box Gift: Encouraging Yourself and Others to Pray* (by Dru Scott Decker, San Francisco: BridgeCross Press, 2001). As a happily married woman today, what a privilege it is to be able to share these powerful and practical ways to build your relationship with God and your family. If you can finish praying for yourself, your family, and the world in two or three minutes, you will enjoy these quick and easy ways that prompt you to pray Scripture and turn earthquake prayers during an emergency into tapestry prayers woven throughout your day.

"B" for Reading the Bible

> But He answered and said, "It is written, 'Man shall not live on bread alone, but on every word that proceeds out of the mouth of God'" (Matthew 4:4 NASB).

In addition to praying and talking to God, we need the other side of communication—listening to God. And the best way to listen to God and receive His guidance is by reading the Bible daily. You may read for only a few minutes or for several hours. The key is to ask God to show you what He wants you to know, learn, or use. Read until there is a gentle lifting of an idea. Something that has special relevance to you. Mark it in your Bible to help you focus on it. If nothing stands out, ask God to plant His Word in your heart anyway. We know that time reading and studying the Bible is an investment for today and the future.

> Your word is a lamp to my feet and a light for my path (Psalm 119:105).

What Happens When You Spend 15 Minutes a Day Reading the Bible?

When I recommend reading the Bible through each year, people often answer with two objections. The first one is usually, "I don't have time." There is a sigh of relief when they hear that it only takes 15 minutes a day.

The second objection is this: "But there are things in the Bible I don't understand." This objection was answered for me one night as I pushed open the door, hesitated, and then stepped into a Conservatory of Music class on singing the Messiah. My musical background was minuscule. My hesitation grew when the registration card asked each person to check soprano, alto, tenor, or bass. I was sure about the squares for tenor and bass, but I didn't know about the squares for soprano or alto.

Before I had decided, a staff member at the next table handed me a book with music for the Messiah. As I opened the inch-thick book and looked at one page, more musical notes than I could count stared back.

One question kept running through my mind, "What am I doing here?" But I decided to table my fear and trust a friend's enthusiasm about the teacher's class from the last Christmas season.

When I found a seat, a feeling of relief settled over me as teacher Michael Matson stood by the piano and welcomed the group with this message: "Remember the goal of this class. No matter what your musical skill is today, you are here to enjoy the *Messiah* and get more notes every year."

Get More Notes Every Year

The same message is true for reading the Bible. Gain more meaning every time. Don't hesitate reading it because you don't understand everything. The riches of God's Word will continue to provide guidance and unveil the mystery of knowing your Creator. Each time you open the Bible, pray and ask God to show you what He wants you to do. Read the Bible through each year and remember the secret: Get more notes every year.

In addition to your daily reading, reach for other resources for your questions. Ask your pastor. Ask the people who teach Bible study classes. Visit your favorite Christian bookstore and ask for commentaries that will give you more insight. As you continue to explore the Bible each day, you will find it a treasure chest of practical and inspiring ideas.

Invest 15 minutes a day and you can read the Bible through in a year. Remember the power of Do It Daily.

"C" for the Character of God

> For this reason we have always prayed for you....We ask God to fill you with the knowledge of his will, with all the wisdom and understanding that his Spirit gives. Then you will be able to live as the Lord wants and always do what pleases him. Your lives will produce good deeds, and you will grow in your knowledge of God (Colossians 1:9,10 TEV).

In going back to the pattern of P for prayer, B for Bible reading, and C for seeking to understand the character of God, you may be asking, "Why should I spend time understanding the character of God?" Although there are many benefits, the one that surprises people is that when you understand the character of God, you can erase a number of items from your to-do list. Consider these three:

1. Feeling resentful for the way someone treated you. Getting even is not on your list. It's on God's list. God says:

   > It is mine to avenge; I will repay (Deuteronomy 32:35).

2. Feeling like a failure. We read that God is a God of hope and new beginnings.

   > Praise be to the God and Father of our Lord Jesus Christ! In His great mercy he has given us new birth into a living hope through the resurrection of Jesus Christ from the dead (1 Peter 1:3).

3. Feeling totally alone. The Bible assures us that the Lord is our shepherd, comforter, and strong deliverer.

   > The Lord is my Shepherd, I shall not be in want. He makes me lie down in green pastures, he leads me beside quiet waters, he restores my soul. He guides me in paths of righteousness for his name's sake. Even though I walk through the valley of the shadow of death, I will fear no evil, for you are with me; your rod and your staff, they comfort me. You prepare a table before me in the presence of my enemies. You anoint my head with oil, my cup overflows. Surely goodness and love will follow me all the days of my life, and I will dwell in the house of the LORD forever (Psalm 23:1-6).

When Elizabeth gave me a mug with a shepherd and a sheep on it, she didn't know it would start my collection of sheep mugs. When another friend, Crissie, gave me a book about sheep, she didn't know it would bring tears to my eyes as I turned the pages. It explained the character and actions of a loving shepherd guiding sheep and what sheep were like. In *A Shepherd Looks at Psalm 23*, Philip Keller explained what can happen to a sheep who does not have a moment-by-moment relationship with its shepherd. A sheep will often keep digging his nose into the dirt to find grass where it used to be and no longer is. A sheep can lay down, accidentally roll on its back with legs kicking in the air, and not be able to right itself. Or a sheep can follow a misguided leader to the edge of a cliff and over.

A sheep needs a good shepherd for constant guidance. That must be why Jesus tells us in John's Gospel, "I am the good shepherd. The good shepherd lays down his life for the sheep" (John 10:11). Can you imagine a sheep telling its shepherd, "See you later if I have a big problem," and then running off alone to the next field? Like that sheep, we need guidance from our Good Shepherd in a day-by-day, moment-by-moment relationship.

When you want to know items that should not be on your to-do list and items that should be on it, look to your Good Shepherd. Turn your to-do list into your prayer list. Look to answers from God in a relationship with God. Grow in your knowledge of Him and His character.

PBC and Doing It Daily

> O, Lord, be gracious to us; we long for you. Be our
> strength every morning (Isaiah 33:2).

Not one person has taken me aside after a presentation to question me about the value of daily prayer, Bible reading, and seeking to know more of the character of God. However, dozens of people have questioned me about how to keep consistent in a daily appointment with God. And that's an area where I used to struggle until this simple process emerged. People who use this idea hug me and thank me because it is so simple and powerful.

Here it is. Buy a calendar that shows the entire year on one sheet and put it in some place where other people in your life will see it. The family room, the wall over a telephone, your work area at home, someplace where both you and others will see it. Then each day when you finish your time of prayer, Bible study, and seeking to know the character of God, walk over to that calendar and write PBC on that date. You can see already how motivating this process is. There is only one day a year when you can write something in the square for today, yet you and others get to look at the calendar for an entire year! And your family and friends will look.

Here's an inspiring variation. Jane started investigating the Bible, trusted Christ, and then longed for her husband to love Jesus. Her zealous recommendations for her husband were not well received. She was discouraged, but kept praying. Then as she was standing in their bathroom, she looked at the wall by the door, and said, "That's where it goes." She hung a monthly calendar, kept praying for her husband, kept applying what God was teaching her, stopped saying anything about church, Jesus, or the Bible, and wrote PBC in each day she did them all. Before three months had passed, her husband asked her about it and decided he wanted to adopt the PBC practice too. Within six months of starting his PBC habit, he asked a friend at breakfast how he could get right with God.

If you struggle with consistency in your daily appointment with God, you are welcome to use or adapt the yearly calendar tool. You will be delighted with the results, and you'll be ready for the secret of more strength in your time.

Chapter 25

Be Compared to a Wise Builder

Therefore everyone who hears these words of Mine and acts on them, may be compared to a wise man who built his house on the rock.

Matthew 7:24 NASB

Treasure what God is showing you in the Bible. Be compared to a wise man who built his house on a rock. Hear God's Word and act on it. Here's a simple way to help you do this. Ask God, "How do You want me to respond to what I have read today?" If you pray this and pause for a moment, an action idea will usually come to your mind. Check to make sure that the action idea is consistent with what you have read through all your reading of the Bible. Then gain the house-on-a-rock benefit—hearing the words of God and acting on them.

When I first asked Jesus to be the Lord of my life, I had no idea how this spiritual transformation and acting on what I read in the Bible would change my complicated relationship with my mother.

When Addison-Wesley published my first book, I could hardly wait to have them send a copy to her. I imagined she would say that this accomplishment was important and that I was important. Or she might become a cheerleader and wave pom-poms. But she didn't.

Even though she had little formal education, she was the only person I knew who had read the entire bookshelf of Harvard Classics. Not only once, but twice. So I can somewhat understand her thinking when she received the copy of my non-classic, nuts-and-bolts book. But I still felt devastated when I called and her first comment was, "Who would buy a book like that?"

Even after that comment, I intellectually knew she loved me. After all, she baked my favorite crunchy oatmeal cookies, clipped articles and sent them to me, and helped me start buying my own home. But I still wanted her to say the words, "I love you, and I'm proud of you."

Even with all I knew, I still ended up not calling or visiting her very often. Yet as I read the Bible, prayed, and ask for God's guidance, the spotlight was on my behavior, and I knew it wasn't right. By this time my mother had suffered three heart attacks and was limited in what she could do and where she could go, so I needed to drive the 90 miles to see her. But I still didn't apply what God was showing me.

Then one evening as I was running in place on the small trampoline in my utility room, I prayed the Bible quote over and over that begins, "Our Father, who is in heaven."

Before very many minutes passed, an insight opened my heart. I stopped running in place, stepped off the little trampoline, and said out loud in amazement:

"My mother and I have the same heavenly Father. I have unconditional love from Him. I don't need to keep trying to drag it out of her."

Rather than continuing to figuratively grasp my mother by the collar and demand that she give me the unconditional love I wanted—in the way I wanted it—I knew that I had been given a rich supply of God's unconditional love. So I stopped trying to reattach my umbilical cord to my mother and realized that it was now attached to my heavenly Father.

It was a toss-up whether my mother or I was happier with this change in me. As I started calling her daily and seeing her more often, I started understanding how she did the best she could with what she had. My job was not to try and change her; it was to keep hearing God's Word and applying what God was showing me in my life. It was to be compared to a wise man who built his house on a rock.

Not too much later, Elizabeth started encouraging me to use the next key to spiritual growth.

Chapter 26

Be a Three-List Person

*Yet to all who received him, to those who believed in his name,
he gave the right to become children of God.*

John 1:12

When you read the story at the beginning of this book about
my neighbor and friend who prayed for me, loved me, and
helped me find answers in the Bible, you didn't know something
in the back of her mind that is now in the front of my organizer.
Three lists. They are titled: New Daily Readers of the Bible, New
Seekers of Christ, and New Fishers of Men.

Here are the specifics about the three lists.

List 1: New Daily Readers of the Bible

At the top of this list, I place the people whom I have encouraged and who are reading something in the Bible daily. What a
privilege to pray for them to continue in this enriching daily
practice.

On the bottom of this list are those whom I am encouraging
to start reading something in the Bible daily. The Bible is a treasure chest of wisdom and guidance. Because this was a life-
lifting practice for me, and because this only takes a few minutes
a day, and because it helps us understand God's love for each of
us individually, I'm always waving the banner for reading something in the Bible daily. Even if a person doesn't believe in the
Bible, it's worth reading to know what this book says. After all, it

has influenced people around the world for centuries. No matter what my activity, what a delight it is to find a place to share this passion.

List 2: New Seekers of Christ

At the top of this list I write the names of people whom I have encouraged to trust God, to confess to God that they have fallen short of His design for them, to accept that they can never do enough good things to earn His love, to ask for forgiveness, and to pray and ask Jesus to come into their hearts as Lord and Savior and fill them with His peace and power.

On the bottom of this list I place each spiritual seeker God has given me a special love for. This means doing for them what Elizabeth did for me: praying daily. Praying for hurts and hopes. Loving consistently. Praying for questions that would give me an opportunity to open the Bible and and show the answers.

List 3: Fishers of Men

At the top of this list, I put the names of people whom I have encouraged and who are experiencing the joy of helping others trust Jesus as Lord.

On the bottom of this list are the names of people who are special in my life, who follow Christ but have not yet encouraged a spiritual seeker to know the joy of trusting Christ as Savior and Lord.

This passion, purpose, and organizing principle in my life today adds joy beyond my imagination. It helps me say no and yes at the right time. It helps me know where to go. It gives me energy for prayer. It gives me the drive to polish and finish this book.

When another friend sat down over breakfast at a little café, I had never thought of what the last instructions were that Jesus gave to His disciples. I had known that the last thing parents tell their children as they go out the door is often what they most want them to remember and do. But when my friend opened the Bible and pointed to the end of the book of Matthew, the message was clear. Make disciples.

> Then Jesus came to them and said, "All authority in heaven and on earth has been given to me. Therefore go and make disciples of all nations, baptizing them in the name of the Father and of the Son and of the Holy Spirit, and teaching them to obey everything I have commanded you. And surely I am with you always, to the very end of the age" (Matthew 28:18-20).

Throughout this book, you have been given practical tools that anyone can select from and use. But the real power to use them fully comes from God. You have heard how the only priorities that will satisfy are the ones that please Him. And you don't have to spend any time wondering if being a three-list person will please God. It will. As you read of my love and gratitude to my friend Elizabeth who prayed for me and discipled me, you don't have to wonder if being a three-list person will make you loved. It will. You don't have to wonder if this is a life purpose that will satisfy you for the years to come. It will. When Elizabeth reached out to me, she gave a gift beyond measure. How could I not want to give to others and help them read the Bible daily and trust Jesus Christ as Lord?

This outreach became my life's priority and passion and later a class and book titled: *When People You Love Don't Love Jesus* (by Dru Scott Decker, San Francisco: BridgeCross Press, 2001).

Whatever resources you use, be a three-list person. It will help you find time because it gives you joy and energy. Be a three-list person. It will help you find time because you know how you can serve the people in your daily life. Be a three-list person. It will help you lay up treasure in heaven that will be gold, silver, and precious stones.

You can read more about practical tools for making disciples in *When People You Love Don't Love Jesus* or you can have the book's strategy in a sentence: Pray, love, and answer questions. Be a three-list person.

Chapter 27

The Do-It-Daily Secret
for Finding More Time

Then he said to them all: "If anyone would come after me,
he must deny himself and take up his cross daily and follow me."
Luke 9:23

As I was reading through the Bible one year, this sentence and the word "daily" touched me. Daily is what makes the difference in so many arenas of life. We've all seen examples of this. The person with flash but no faithfulness does not gain the results of the person who faithfully continues in the right direction.

Why does doing something daily release so much power? And how could a small amount of time each day produce such large results? Those questions were on my mind as I read the Bible.

The story of Samson (Judges 13–16) intrigued me. Samson—with all his power and strength—was eventually defeated by Delilah. But Delilah didn't topple him through her own physical strength, and it wasn't because she had a good goal. It was through the power she gained by doing it daily. Delilah defeated strong Samson when she asked him *daily* what the source of his strength was.

For several more months, gaining wisdom stayed my special focus in reading the Bible. So one day when I opened my Bible to the book of Proverbs and read chapter 8, I drew a square around verses 32 through 35. They spoke the power of "do it daily" to me.

> Do as I say, and you will be happy. Listen to what you are taught. Be wise; do not neglect it. The man who listens to me will be happy—the man who stays at my door every day, waiting at the entrance to my home. The man who finds me finds life, and the Lord will be pleased with him (Proverbs 8:32-35 TEV).

That was the secret: "The man who listens to me will be happy—the man who stays at my door every day..." I stopped in the middle of the sentence as the words "stays at my door every day" jumped off the page. That was it. To gain wisdom, I needed to stay at the door, to read God's Word every day. I needed to do it daily.

Occasionally, the image of my father comes to my mind, and I remember him working at his carpentry table as I sat on the low wooden bench he had built for my four-year-old legs. When I remember him asking me to hold a board steady while he sawed, I knew he was happy with me.

In later years, even though he had died, I knew he would not have been happy with some things I was doing. However, when I confessed how my life missed the mark of what God had designed for me, believed that Jesus loved me individually, and accepted that He died on the cross to pay for my wrongdoing, even though my father did not live to see that day, he would have been delighted with that decision.

And I look forward to the time when I can talk with him—and my mother—about what they gave my life in their example of faithfulness—doing it daily—doing the right things at the right times—with God's power.

> His master replied, "Well done, good and faithful servant!" (Matthew 25:23).

Quick Review

The Strong Foundation

When you want to find more time, don't try to do it alone.

Start with God. Ask Him to be your Coach and "Wonderful Counselor." Ask for God's help, and then follow His guidance.

The Five Sets of Tools

Personality Tools—To help you know your time style so you can pick your time tools

Skip the one-size-fits-all time approaches.

Reach for the few time techniques that fit your personality, priorities, and pressures. Remember your strengths and gifts.

Focusing Tools—For direction and organization

Drop the pressure to get everything done.

Focus on the target of doing the right things at the right times.

Overcoming Tools—To gain energy and get back on the right track

Get help for straying or stalling.

Shepherd your time. Protect it, guide it, and get it back on the path and moving ahead.

Daily Tools—To gain more success with everyday time demands

Don't wait for a fix-everything, win-the-lottery solution.

Gain big improvements with daily steps in the right direction.

Spiritual Tools—To help you enjoy your Coach and Wonderful Counselor

Clean out the idea that spiritual growth is climbing a ladder to God.

Accept the gift of a loving relationship with God and grow in His love and power.

Which Category Am I?

Check Yourself: Do You Have a Category One or Category Two Time Style?

1. Do you have any unopened mail in your office or home that is older than three days?

Yes _____ No _____

2. Is there an article of clothing somewhere in your home that is in a temporary parking place like the floor, a pile in your closet, or tossed across a chair?

Yes _____ No _____

3. During the last week, have you had trouble concentrating because there are so many things running through your mind?

Yes _____ No _____

4. If you were able to add up all the time you've spent searching for objects during the past week—whether for keys, paperwork, clothing, or anything else—would it total more than 30 minutes?

Yes _____ No _____

5. During the last week, have you been late to one or more appointments or commitments?

Yes _____ No _____

6. When on the phone during the last week, have you said even once, "Wait a moment, I have to get something to write with"? Include calls on your cell phone.

Yes _____ No _____

7. During the last week, has someone had to ask you for the same thing more than once?

Yes _____ No _____

8. During the last month, have you found yourself thinking or saying even once that you just spent some time watching something terrible on television?

Yes _____ No _____

9. During the last month, have you forgotten the birthday of a close friend or family member?

Yes _____ No _____

10. Have you at some point during the last month worn any clothes out of your dirty clothes hamper or from a pile of dirty clothes on the floor?

Yes _____ No _____

Now count the number of times you checked yes.

If you checked yes to two or more questions, you can consider yourself a Category Two person in terms of your time. You are ready for the special time tools you will find in this book.

If you checked yes to only one question, you can get by with a few traditional time tools. However, when you pick a new time tool that fits you, you are living up to the old saying, "The rich get richer."

Chapter 2: How This Book Can Help You

1. Malcolm Gladwell, *The Tipping Point: How Little Things Can Make a Big Difference* (New York: Little, Brown and Company, 2000), pp. 1-10.

Chapter 9: The Few Techniques That Free You from Compulsive Time

1. Taibi Kahler, Ph.D., with Hedges Capers, Div.M., "The Miniscript," in *Transactional Analysis Journal*, IV, I, January 1974, pp. 26-42.

List of Figures

Chapter 6: Your Stimulation and Excitement Quota and Your Time

Robert L. Goulding, M.D., and Mary McClure Goulding, M.S.W., *The Power Is in the Patient* (San Francisco: TA Press, 1978).

Chapter 9: The Few Techniques That Free You from Compulsive Time

Taibi Kahler, Ph.D., *The Mastery of Management: Or, How to Solve the Mystery of Mismanagement* (Little Rock, AR: Kahler Communications, Inc., 2000).

Robert S. Maris, Ph.D., *The Great Design: A Personality Profile from the Christian Worldview Based on the Kahler Process Communication Model* (Little Rock, AR: Servants by Design, 2000). ServantsByDesign.com

Chapter 10: What to Carve Out When There's Too Much to Do

Garry Friesen, *Decision Making and the Will of God: A Biblical Alternative to the Traditional View* (Portland, OR: Multnomah Press, 1980).

J. Edward Russo and Paul J. H. Schoemaker, *Decision Traps: Ten Barriers to Brilliant Decision-Making and How to Overcome Them* (New York: Fireside Books, Simon & Schuster, 1989).